At 100
Her Children Rise Up and Call Her
Blessed!

EMMA JANE ROWLAND

In Honor of her Love, her Life and her Legacy.

Compiled By
Cheryl Pope Clark

AT 100 HER CHILDREN RISE UP AND CALL HER BLESSED!

Copyright © 2015 by Cheryl Pope Clark

Second printing – October 2016

Published by C3 Enterprise

All rights reserved. No part of this book may be reproduced or transmitted in any form or by any means without written permission from the author.

I am deeply grateful to the following individuals for the professional services they rendered, in excellence, and their loving support for this book project. My prayer is that God continues to bless each of you and enlarge your territories, in Jesus' name, Amen.

Book Jacket Design by Christopher Hayes, Amalgamated Pixels

Photoshoot Coordinator – Cynthia Harper

Photography by Lloyd Caldway, APV Images

Make Up by Deidre Brown Beauty

Mother Rowland's Wardrobe courtesy of Joyce Rowland

Mother Rowland's Beauty Consultants – Thesa Long and Sara Robbins

Publishing Consultants – Lakeisha Dixon
                                   Stephan Labossiere
                                   Tracey Redding Smith

Edits (2016) by Verna Colson and Christian Clark

Layout services by Ya Ya Ya Creative, www.yayayacreative.com

Project Consultant – Pastor Christopher Boyd

Audio Production – James and Regina Howard "A Sound Voice"*
*ONLINE BOOK PURCHASES: The accompanying audio CD is available to buy. Contact C3 Enterprise at c3getaways@gmail.com.

ISBN No. 978-0-9967303-1-0

PRINTED AND BOUND IN THE UNITED STATES OF AMERICA

Dedication

This book is dedicated to my Grandmother, Emma Jane Rowland.

According to Ancestry.com:

> *"In general we think of a generation being about 25 years - from the birth of a parent to the birth of a child. We also generally accept that the length of a generation in earlier periods of history was closer to 20 years when humans mated younger and life expectancies were shorter."*

She has been a strong matriarch of the family for many generations; four with my mother and five with her son Jim's daughter, Francine Pope. Even with that, our local family is relatively small and there have been adopted daughters and sons in our lives for as far back as seventy-five years. These adopted children refer to her as "Mother" and if you go way back, it's "Mama" and they do what children do. They call, visit, cook, clean house, buy meals and groceries, buy clothes, purchase computers, take her to church, take her on trips, take her to get her hair and nails done, take her on doctor's appointments, take her on errands or run them for her, take her to the movies and concerts, plant trees in the yard, mow the lawn, perform odd jobs around the house, install driveway rails, paint the house, send flowers, candy, cakes, and money! They do things that don't always get acknowledged, but are appreciated nevertheless.

She is so special to so many people and the appreciation and honor that is given to her is just amazing. This book gives a small glimpse of who she is and how much she means to her "children".

Table of Contents

Foreword 1
Preface 3
Message from Mother 4
Contributing Writers 5

Mamama
Chapter 1 – *Emma Jane Rowland* 9

The Interview
Chapter 2 – *The Interview* 15

Natural Born Leader
Chapter 3 – *Woman of Integrity* 35
Chapter 4 – *Always Learning* 37
Chapter 5 – *Faith* 39

Tribute to Our Mother
Tribute to Mother 43

Family
Family Testimonials 47

Friends
Friends Tributes 69

Neighbor
Neighbors Acclaim 79

The Help
The Helps Praise 83

Faith
Faith Testimonies 91

Foreword
for Rev. Emma Rowland
By
Bishop Dale C. Bronner

Rev. Emma Rowland is a gift from God who has lived to see the faithfulness of God down through the generations! It is a joy to witness the Christ-like character of Jesus exhibited through her genteel demeanor. She has a unique gift of teaching the Word of God with clarity and simplicity. Her honesty rings through with great practicality.

As I reminisce on her bountiful life, I am reminded of the words of the psalmist in Psalm 92:

> [12] *The righteous shall flourish like a palm tree,*
> *He shall grow like a cedar in Lebanon.*
>
> [13] *Those who are planted in the house of the Lord*
> *Shall flourish in the courts of our God.*
>
> [14] *They shall still bear fruit in old age;*
> *They shall be fresh and flourishing,*
>
> [15] *To declare that the Lord is upright; He is my rock, and*
> *there is no unrighteousness in Him.*

Yes, Rev. Emma Rowland has continued to bear fruit in old age. She is the personification of this scripture! She is a witness that God is our dwelling place in all generations (Ps. 90:1). Our world is better because our lives have had the privilege of overlapping with her beautiful life and ministry! I celebrate her love, her life, her legacy!

Preface

The Lord laid it on my heart many years ago to write a book about my grandmother and I said, "Okay Lord that's a great idea!" and I did nothing. He said it again during a time when I was unemployed and had all the time in the world to do it and again I said, "Okay Lord, this is a great time, I'll do it!" and again, I did nothing. Early in June of this year, a friend of mine who also happens to be many things to me including my personal prayer intercessor, my life coach and business partner, asked the question, "Do you have a book on the inside of you screaming to get out?" I replied, "I wish I did but unfortunately I don't!" Do you know how fast the Holy Spirit arrested me?? He said, "I told you what to write years ago and I need you to write it NOW!" This time I said, "Yes Lord I hear you LOUD and CLEAR and I will do it!" Fortunately, this same friend, Lakeisha Dixon, who is also a multiple streams entrepreneur, was scheduling an online seminar on how to write and publish a book in 90 days and I signed up!

I knew I had to hold myself accountable to this charge by making a public announcement of my intentions and I did. On July 13, 2015, I began sending out notices to her pastors, family, and close friends letting them know what God had called me to do and that I needed their help! I knew I couldn't do this on my own and I politely told the Lord this is HIS PROJECT and I am just a willing vessel to use to get what He wants published.

I thank God and ALL OF YOU for your contributing chapters and tributes. When I began to feel overwhelmed, He reminded me He was there and you all encouraged me with your words of support! This has truly been a labor of love and one that I am SO GLAD the Lord trusted me with. When I began to delve into the project and begin to receive all of your submissions, it became more and more clear as to why this project is necessary.

I love you Mamama! ♡

Message from Mother
(with her shouting shoes on)

I've had my share of life's ups and downs
God's been good to me, and the downs have been few
I would guess you can say, God has blessed me
But there's never been a time in my life, he didn't bring me through.

If anyone should ever write, my life story.
For whatever reason there might be.
You'd be there, between each line of pain and glory.

Jesus is the best thing that ever happened...
Jesus is the best thing that ever happened...
Jesus is the best thing that ever happened to me.

If anyone should ever write, my life story.
For whatever reason there might be.
One day, I was lost but Jesus found me.

If anyone should ever write, my life story.
For whatever reason there might be.
I was on my way to hell, but Jesus reached down and grabbed me, Hallelujah!

Lyrics courtesy of Rev. James Cleveland

Contributing Writers
(Listed in Alphabetical Order)

Alice Evans
Annie Mae Stublefield
Bettye Hunter
Bishop Dale C. & Dr. Nina D. Bronner
Blanche Mills
Calina Clark
Cameron Taylor
Charlie, Pat and Brent Davis
Christian Clark
Clarissa Flowers
Crystal Walker-Banks
Curtis Harris
Curtis Minter
Cynthia Harper
Deacon Johnnie and Beverly Simmons
Deacon Steve and Karen Bradfield
Denise C. Pope
Don Vellek and Manny Beauregard
Donella P. Cantrell
Doris Davis
Dorothy Cobb
Dr. Jane Render
Dr. Prince Martin, Jr. and Dr. Frances Martin
Dr. Susan Bailey
Dr. Linda Chinn
Elder Minnie Taylor
Elizabeth O'Connell
Florence Jackson
Forrestine Lewis Hightower
Gloria Buchanan
Gloria Lloyd
Gloria Weaver
Gwen Walker
Ivory Dorsey
Jerome Ragsdale
Jerri Sullivan
Joan Hadley
Joyce Rowland
Joyce Simpson
Julia Thomas
Katherine Thomas

Continued on the next page ...

Lena Barnes	Rev. Charles Houston
Leola Butler	Rev. W. L. Cottrell, Sr.
Lillian Gray	Robert Lee Carter
Lillie Wade	Rodney Moss
Linda Paulding	Sara Robbins
Mae Battle	Sharon Bradley
Mattie Copeland	Sherry Lavonda Johnson Molden
Mencia Johnson	Stephanie Williams
Minister Mary Bell	Thesa Long
Mirna Oglivie	Tondalaya Woods
Naomi Williams	Tracey Hodges
Nedra Holman	Tracey Smith
Pastor Christopher Boyd	Velma E. Watkins
Paul Patrick	Vera Pope
Queen S. Emory	Vivian Toney
Ramona Battle	Willie, Marva & Jordan Edwards
Reginald Sapp	Zelma S. Harris

Mamama

(Translated MY Grandmama)

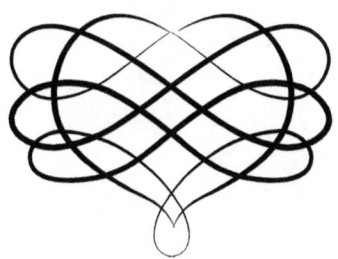

Chapter 1
Emma Jane Rowland

This book is about an extraordinary individual known to many as Mother, known to some as Reverend, and known to me as "Mamama". I am her granddaughter and of the two biological ones that she has, I am the only one who lives in the local area, thus, I have spent the most time in her presence.

Growing up for me included an overnight visit to my grandparent's home every Friday night. Those nights would include watching black and white TV on the floor by my granddads feet while he relaxed in his recliner and Mamama on her sewing machine making an outfit for the week. Mamama was an excellent seamstress and a very stylish dresser. Our weekends would include trips to the fabric store where she would sort through fabric, patterns and accessories for the right outfit, and trips to the Mall, mostly Greenbriar Mall until Cumberland Mall opened, to buy shoes, etc. Sometimes she would give me scrap fabric and she taught me how to cut out and hand sew miniature dresses to keep me occupied.

Growing up with my grandparents was a very special time in my life. They encouraged me to be and do anything my heart desired and they were there to support me through all of it. Mamama was, and still is, a "Road Jane". That means she loves to GO! She always had a nice car because my granddaddy was retired from General Motors so they both had nice cars. Every Sunday that there was a choir anniversary or special program after church, we would be right there. We'd be right in that church just fanning a way because it was always so hot!

For as long as I can remember, she was always a very active and involved member at Beulah Baptist Church where Reverend W. L. Cottrell was the fine pastor. She was a faithful member and president of the Usher Board #1. When it was her Sunday to usher, I watched her every move. She was such an excellent leader. That was the best usher board that church had during that time. Everyone was shown to their seats and they made sure to cover the ladies legs and give them sniffing salts for when they shouted.

We had to be at church early Sunday mornings because she taught Sunday School in the young males, ages 9–12. I noticed that they were a well-mannered group of boys who always seemed eager to be in her class - and on time. After Sunday School was over, she would head to "her seat" which was on the second pew on the left end which was the same pew as the First Family who sat on the right end. I would join her on occasion when my good friend Karen Thomas Woodard did not attend service. If Karen was at church, I would sit in the back with her where we loved to play tic-tac-toe, dot-to-dot and hangman. Please don't tell Reverend Cottrell that we weren't paying attention to his sermons. We could always hear what it was about later that afternoon when our mother's would be on the phone recalling how good service was and what the preacher preached about.

My grandmother loved to "GO" and I was her very present travel companion. We didn't have to 'go' though, in order for me to enjoy my time with her. I would always enjoy listening to her sing gospel songs, talk on the phone or talk to my granddaddy whom we affectionately called G.P. which were his initials for George Parker. I love the story of how they met:

He was working at the General Motors plant in Hapeville, GA and she worked the steam table at Joe's restaurant nearby where a lot of the plant workers had lunch. I felt it was a Divine connection because the only reason she was working at Joe's at that time was because her employer, Scripto, (the pen and lighter manufacturing company) was on strike. He would make small talk when he came through the line. They rode the same bus to work and when she got on, he would get up to give her his seat. He would stand over her, of course. One day she got on and pulled out a bag of Valentine cards to address while in route to work. He told her she sure did have a lot of friends. She explained that she taught Sunday School and the cards were for her students. Soon, they had reached their destination. The next day when she got on the bus, he asked her had she finished her cards. Next thing you know, he was telling her he wanted to get to know her better and did she think it would be okay if he stopped by to visit. She agreed and they set the date for Sunday after church. Well, when Sunday came, Mamama decided she was going to a church where her coworker from Joe's Cafeteria invited her which would delay her return home. She got cold feet.

Needless to say, she wasn't home when he got there. Her children answered the door and told him she wasn't there. He introduced himself to them and gave them each a quarter. They were so excited that when she got home they could barely contain their excitement about this man who had come to see her and had left them quarters! This was surprising that they liked him so soon because the sons, especially, had made it plain and clear that they did not welcome nor need a man in their lives. They would take care of their Mama and didn't need help from "no man". But G.P. was different! He brought quarters! The next day finally rolled around and when she got on the bus he said, "You stood me up!" She said, "Yeah, I stood you up before you could stand me up! She thought he was probably already married and was talking empty words and she didn't want to be disappointed. Eventually though, they did end up dating for about two years before they got married.

They kept their marriage a secret. It was during the time of war and housing was hard to find. They wanted to wait until they could find a place to live before they announced the marriage to anyone.

G.P. was a widower with two children, Marcus and Cecille. Mamama had her three young teenaged children. In the meantime, they were making sure the children spent time with each other getting to know one another and bonding. During their courtship, they were under the watchful eye of my mother, Vera, who at the age of fifteen, accompanied them on their walks in the park and various other locations.

The Interview

Chapter 2
The Interview

Before I write more from my personal perspective, I want to share with you an interview that I had the privilege and honor of conducting with Mamama for StoryCorps at the Atlanta History Center as arranged by Pastor Christopher Boyd of Word of Faith Family Worship Cathedral. It was a wonderful experience to be able to ask her questions about a lot of things and in some cases, just letting her share what was on her heart. The transcript of the interview is as follows:

Me: I am Cheryl Clark. I am 50 years old. Today's date is Tuesday, April 30, 2013. I am in Atlanta, Georgia and I am here with my grandmother, Emma Jane Rowland. Emma Rowland, what is your age?

Mother: I am 96 years old

Me: And today's date?

Mother: April 30, 2013

Me: Your location?

Mother: Atlanta, GA

Me: And your relationship to me?

Mother: Your grandmother

Me: Okay. Well Grandmother we are just thrilled to be here at the Atlanta History Center at StoryCorp, interviewing you with questions that will go down in history for years to come. For generations to come. I would like to thank Pastor Boyd of Word of Faith for this opportunity to be here today. I have a few questions that I started writing down a few years ago. Actually, it was when I considered writing a book about you. In addition to those

| | questions, I reached out to some of my Facebook friends this morning to get more questions to see what they were interested in finding out about you (they all know you from the many posts I share about my wonderful family), as well as questions from your great-grandchildren. So, first off I think we can kind of break the ice a little bit and let you get started to talk about what's on your mind today - what you would like the readers to know about you before we get into the questions and answers. Do you have anything that you would like to just share with the readers? |

Mother: My name is Emma J. Rowland and I am 96 years old. I was born October 9, 1916 to George and Malinda Walton in Stuart County, Georgia. Today, I am excited and it is good to have Pastor Boyd who is one of my favorite people at Word of Faith Church. He is always smiling and always so loving until I just feel perfectly comfortable; and Vera, my only daughter, which I thank God for that, I had three children – two sons and one daughter and my two sons have passed on. I had prayed that God would give me a little girl and He gave me the kind of daughter that I would have selected if I had had the opportunity to do so. Thank you Vera, for being such a precious daughter. Cheryl is her daughter, who is, I can say this since the rest of them are not here (chuckles) my favorite granddaughter (Me: They're going to get you for saying that!) Yeah, and she thinks she owns me and has always been like that. She told me whenever I had to work over time to "tell those people that you have to see about me so you can't work overtime." So even today, she tells me what to do and I obey and so I am glad to be here today and I look forward to answering some questions that she has.

Me: Okay. Well, that's great Grandmother! Some of the first questions, of course is about your childhood - if we can start there a little bit - tell us some things about your home life. I know that I never got to meet your parents or grandparents so if you could just share a little bit about your home life growing up, what were things like before your mother passed and after?

Mother: I was six years old when my mother passed and I can remember us going to church. We lived in the country and my father would get us all on the wagon and we would go to church on Sunday morning. Church life was good as we knew it then and it's so different from what church life is today because the song service we could hear before we arrived at church was so appealing when you arrived and you could hardly wait to get there, to get inside to join in the song service and it was really good – much different from church life now. Although church life today is good, it is just so different and that was a good part of growing up. My mother died when I was six years old and I remember her calling my sister – who was a year older than myself, I am the seventh of nine – and she called us to her bed and told us that her mother would be there in a few days and she wanted us to tell her to take us home with her and raise us just like she raised her. I didn't know what this was all about but she told us that our father wasn't going to want us to go "but just cry and he will let you go". She died that same night or maybe the next night and as I can recall, a few days later, her mother, my grandmother came and we took her off to the side when we got the chance, to tell her what Mama told us (my sister and I). My sister did not want to go because she liked the food that we had at home and I was glad that our grandmother wanted us to come home with her because I liked to go so it didn't matter to me what type of food they had. It was an opportunity to take a trip. I still like to 'go'. So I went home with my grandmother at the age of six. I had learned my alphabets and a lot from the older siblings who took a lot of pangs in teaching me things. So I could read a little bit and with her help, I learned to improve my reading. When it was time to go to school, she would take me through my homework at night and then we had to do a little Bible Study. We had to read something in the Bible because I was what they called a "sensitive child". I couldn't get over losing my mother, questioning "why did she have to die?" So they said I

Papa George

did a lot of crying. Grandmother was real good and she counseled me to the best of her ability. She did a lot of it with the Bible and that's how I fell in love with the Bible and learned to study it, because of my Grandmother's love for the Bible.

Me: I'd like to interject right here Grandmother. I was talking to your great-grands last night about the interview, trying to solicit some questions from them and one of the questions that they had, had to do with religion. Of course, because you were a Minister when they got here that's all they know and they think you came here, being a Christian, knowing Jesus, saved from the womb, but I have heard differently that your mother's death did affect how you felt about the Lord ... Do you mind expounding on that for us a little?

Mother: When my mother died, they used the term "God took her" and then I had something against God. Why did He take my mother? And that grew in me for a few years. So I think that was why I was such a problem to my grandmother as she tried to get me acquainted with Jesus. I felt like God must have had something against me to take my mother. When I would see other children with their mothers, it would bring up the subject all over again. She worked with me and got me interested in reading the Bible for myself and in doing that I found out in scripture that God did love me - which He did care about me and my Mother's death was between her and Him. So it was her time to go and I just had to learn to live without her. My grandmother told me that God would be a father and a mother for me. I didn't understand that, but I kept expecting it to happen and I understood what she was talking about. I escaped a lot of things and I couldn't explain why I escaped that. My grandmother would say that God was taking care of me

With her sister, Pearlie Mae

and that's the reason I didn't get bit by that snake or whatever it was that was attacking me.

Me: Now when you talk about escaping things, I think it is very important that young females, especially those who may be involved in abusive relationships, understand about how God protected you from the abusive relationship that you were in as a young female, wife and mother. If you will just share a little bit about my grandfather that I never knew but my mother's dad and how God delivered you from that abusive situation.

Mother: I was evidently between the ages of sixteen and seventeen years old when I met him because we were not allowed to date until we were sixteen. At our school, they had baseball games and other little games that the boys participated in and we could go and see them play ball. I met my husband Jim Pope at the game and we started a relationship - a courtship that turned into marriage a year later. I was seventeen and he was twenty-four.

Me: But you were a heartbreaker too, right? He wasn't the only suitor for you at that time?

Mother: Oh no, I had a lot of boyfriends *(chuckling)*!

Me: I know a lot of people would be surprised to hear that!

Mother: I had a lot of boyfriends! I was engaged to two fellas when I got married. My two favorite boyfriends. We did our courting at home sitting in our living room talking, with my grandmother sitting on the front porch or somewhere close by. We had to talk loud or very quiet so we planned marriage and I had these two boyfriends that I liked very much so I had to make a choice between the two so I chose Jim and we got married probably a year later.

Me: What was life like with him?

Mother: It turned out very bad, nobody was married but me. You know, he kept living the kind of life he was living before we got married and I was supposed to have the babies, stay home and take care of the house. He did what he wanted and it turned into a very rough relationship. There was no fighting; he didn't fight me.

	Although he did try one time, I frightened him and let him know I wasn't going to live like that. I had seen my aunts get into violent relationships where they were fighting and I wasn't going to live my life like that. So the one time that he did hit me, I boiled water and threatened to scald him; consequently, he was afraid to go to sleep. So he never tried that again but he did it with his mouth - with verbal abuse.
Me:	Thankfully, you were able to get away from that relationship with three young children.
Mother:	Right. Well, I had learned to trust this God that at first I was afraid of ... I had learned to trust in GOD and I prayed. I had learned to pray and to read the Bible and believe the Bible and to believe that God would do what He said and He did. He delivered me out of that marriage and I felt like I could take care of my children because I didn't mind working and I knew if I got to a place where I could get a job, we could make it. That was my prayer – for God to lead me to a place where I could take care of my children; and my prayer was that He would keep us from begging or stealing and that I could make a living for us and He did that, too! Again, I thanked God that they all did well.
Me:	Praise God! Yes, I know that story and I know that it's a little long for radio; so we'll have to save it for another time. What a lot of people want to know is, since you've been here for 96 years you've seen a lot of advancement in technology and all types of things, do you remember the first time you watched TV?
Mother:	Yes, but that was long after my childhood because we had – [we didn't have a radio]. We had a phonograph. Of course, there was no such thing as electricity and batteries so, it had a crank. We cranked it up and played records, we could get all kinds of records, uh, spiritual, the blues, and all kinds. So we listened to that. There was no radio, which was the only music we had back then. Other than that, some of us learned how to play the organ and/or piano or other musical instruments. We had an organ at the house. I never learned to play the organ but that's what we had for music and entertainment.

Me: Okay, so you all had parties back then and someone was assigned to crank the phonograph up?

Mother: Right, somebody was assigned to take care of the music and like I said, we had all kinds of music and we would dance at the parties. It was limited to how long it would last and who could attend the party, but we had fun, you know, the kind of fun that we had in those days ... They told jokes and played games like checkers and hopscotch and jackstones - you probably don't know what that is ...

Me: Oh yes, I did that as a young girl and kids still play hopscotch and jackstones these days, at least mine did. Wow, those games have lasted through a lot of time. I didn't know they went that far back!

Now what do you remember about your siblings? You said you were the seventh of nine?

Mother: Right. After my mother passed and I left to go live with my grandmother I didn't see my siblings again for quite a few years. When my two older brothers got old enough, they visited me and; my older sister visited me.

Me: What were their names?

Mother: My older sister was the oldest sibling and her name was Pearlie Mae. My older brother's name was Rayfield and my next brother was George Alexander. They visited me at Grandmother's house when they grew up. I did not see the rest of them until I was grown. I had my first child, went back to see them, and we got acquainted with each other. We just had good times with each other for the rest of the years they were here. They have all passed away – I'm the only one left. But while they lived, we visited one another and had good times together. We talked about the years we were separated and sometimes I was glad that we were separated because we were raised so differently. They had a stepmother and I didn't. My grandmother was so different from their stepmother.

Me: So looking back, you really appreciate the childhood you had?

Mother: Yes (she exclaims with joy!) When I think about it, I say, "Thank you Lord" that I did go live with my grandmother.

Me: That's wonderful. Now your siblings, children, and grandchildren - do you know where any of them are? Do you keep up with any of your siblings' children?

Mother: Yes, my oldest sister's daughter lives in Chicago. She has four children so I know where they are. I hear from them, and she had a son, he passed away and didn't have any children. My oldest brother has a son who lives in Athens, GA. Right now, he is pastoring a church in Athens. I don't know the name of it, but I know it's Pentecostal and his name is Clifford Walton. We talk about once a week - he promised me he would call me about once a week and most times he does. There were a lot of them. I know his older sister lives in California now - her name is Betty. Another one named Deborah, that was just at my house two weeks ago, lives in Alabama. She has a daughter that lives somewhere in Georgia so whenever she is nearby, she will either call or if she has time she will come by and pay me a visit.

Me: Oh, that is so nice that you're still connected with them!

So, you have three children. You've acknowledged my mother, Vera Pope, and what about your two sons?

Mother: Jim passed away in the spring of 1996. We found him dead in his apartment. I know when I saw him that previous Christmas, he was sick. He claimed he was seeing a doctor but he shut himself off and no one had really talked to him or seen much of him. After we couldn't reach him, we reached out to friends who saw him regularly, but they had not heard from him either. A friend of his said she went by to visit him two weeks before we discovered him dead, but he would not allow her to come into the house. He told her he had to get right with his Maker and of course she didn't know what he was talking about - all my children had been taught about God. I taught them to the best of my ability and read the Bible with them and we went to Church very often so much until one of them said when he got grown he was never going to Church because he had been so much in his youth; but he was saved. I know he was Saved because I lead him to Christ myself. I didn't trust what he claimed that he had. He visited me and he was having problems and I said "what you need is Jesus so get on your knees" and I gave him the Bible, turned to Romans 10:9,10 and had him read it. I asked him did he believe what it said and he said "yes". At home, if they were playing music that they knew I didn't approve of, they watched for me when I would get off from work; they'd be on the "look out" for me. They called me "Rev." because I always talked about the Bible. Jim was very lively and funny but he always called me "Rev."

Me: I see. What about your other son?

Mother: Homer and my oldest son were so different from each other. Whereas Jim was very outgoing and had a lot of friends, his brother was very quiet and he died of cancer in 2006 at the Veterans Hospital in Decatur, GA. They were very opposite. Homer was quiet and they called him a "Mama's Boy" because he stayed around me as much as possible. He got married but it didn't work out so he came back home and when he went to the hospital sick he was living at my house. We had a very close relationship.

Me: Now, your daughter Vera was known as the "Boss" so I've heard?

Mother: Yes, indeed! She kept them straight and when she pushed them too hard they called her "fat" because she was kind of chubby (laughter) and when they wanted to get next to her they would call her "fat" but other times they called her boss. They very seldom called her Vera because she would tell them "you get back here and pick up your shoes" trying to make them do right like make up their bed and keep their room cleaned and so they fussed about it but they would do what she told them to do. Sometimes she was "Mama, Jr." because she kept order in the house. You know how she has to have order, right?

Me: Yes I sure do!

Mother: Things had to be neat and in order and she made them pick up after themselves, but when she made them mad they would say "okay FAT" thinking that would make her hush but it didn't bother her.

Me: Thinking back over the years, I know we have had a lot of historical moments lately. What have been some of the first historical moments growing up? (Note to reader, Mother did NOT answer this question as asked – smile)

Mother: We celebrated the Fourth of July and Memorial Day. Those were great holidays for us because on those holidays the schools got together and those baseball teams would play on the field and the grown-ups would set up tables and barbeque on those holidays and we would have a great time celebrating.

Me: Okay those were very memorable times for you then. What about historical? I know there is a new movie out called 42 about the life and times of Jackie Robinson. Were you a sports fan at all? Do you remember Jackie Robinson and Hank Aaron when they integrated the sports leagues or any significant strides made during the civil rights era?

Mother: Jackie Robinson, his name was in everybody's mouth. Everyone was talking about him and by now we had radio and we could hear the ballgames on the radio and he was the topic of a lot of conversations. There was a little tune they had out about "did you see Jackie Robinson hit that ball?" I didn't see him or Hank Aaron on TV at that time. We just had radio. I wasn't a sports fan though so when we did have TV I enjoyed watching Christian broadcasting.

Me: When I did reach out to social media, this morning on Facebook, there were a few questions that were put before me to ask you. One of was "based on all that you've seen in your life, how did you feel when Barack Obama was elected as the first African American President?

Mother: Happy, surprised because I never thought I would live to see a Black person advance that far so I'm still happy about that now, still excited about that. During the time of Martin Luther King, Jr. I was very proud of him the way that he broke down the segregation – that's something that I really appreciate him for doing.

Me: Yes, we have come a long way. We have street names named after a lot of African Americans that have paved the way, we have Joseph E. Lowery Blvd over on what was once called Ashby Street that you're very familiar with.

What about your work life? Tell us about what you grew up doing and talk to us about work ethic a little bit.

Mother: I grew up on the farm where we picked cotton (I interjected "you picked cotton, Grandmama?") yes, I picked cotton. I was little but they let me go to the field and I was afraid of bugs and worms and all kind of things but they let us go to the field when there was no one around to take care of children. We would go and sit under the shade tree and sometimes experience picking cotton. I remember when my grandmother gave me my first bag to pick cotton with it was a little cotton sack and it was made with a strap on the shoulder that you would put over your shoulder and you would pick the cotton and put it in the bag. I didn't do very good at that because I was afraid of everything and there were bugs and worms on the cotton and so that wasn't pleasant.

Me: Ummhmm, I see. Well, let me switch streams a little bit - I know growing up, I've always known you as a Christian Woman and as I mentioned earlier, I just turned 50 and I also mentioned that that's all the girls know – they think that's how you came here and I appreciate how over the years you've lead me to my relationship with God, making sure that when we were in the Baptist Church that we were there every Sunday. You taught Sunday School and every choir anniversary we were there – you loved good Gospel music and after we got into the Non-denominational arena, you made sure we were in a Bible teaching Church and I really appreciate that because I am able to pass that on to my daughters as well. We have mentioned the fact that Pastor Boyd is here on behalf of Word of Faith where you have been a member for quite some time. I remember times, before Bishop Bronner had a Church, you would go to the hotel meetings with him and have just been a faithful follower of his ministry from the very beginning and I would like to say how much your family appreciates how they (Word of Faith Church) have enveloped you and loved on you and made sure that you have been well taken care of and I want to talk about, in the last few minutes that we have, your purpose in life. I know that you have a Ministry for Women – just talk a little bit about your purpose and then end with what you would say to your great grands; what you would like to pass on to them. But first, talk about your purpose and your ministry.

Mother: Ok, my purpose is to teach the Word of God. There were times when there were street preachers downtown and I would catch the bus and between buses you would run into a street preacher on this corner and one on the other corner and they were passing out tracts and I was on my way to the next bus (we had street cars at first) and as they would be passing out tracts, people would be throwing them down and I would be picking them up, on my way to work, and stuff them in my purse and then when I would get a chance, at home at night, I would unload my purse and read tracts and that's how I kept up with Bible Study. I would pick up one and it seemed like every one of them said "Study to show thyself approved unto God, a workman that need not to be ashamed, rightly dividing the Word of Truth, 2 Tim 2:15. I felt like God was telling me something, so I started enrolling in to Bible Classes that I would read about and that were advertised in the paper and one that I signed up for was on Nelson Street where there was a Minister there teaching the Bible class and I signed up for corresponding courses for Bible Study and I felt like God was telling me something and then one day He made it plain to me that He wanted me to – and this is how He said it, "I want you to take My Word to the people" and I thought "God the people I know don't allow women in their Churches preaching". He didn't answer me right then but I went and talked to my Pastor about it and he said God didn't call women to preach, but I knew what God had told me, He wanted me to take His Word to the people and I went back to God with this and He showed me a vision of this tall man, the tallest man I'd ever seen said to me "follow me" and we were entering a garden and this garden had all kinds of flowers in all colors blossoming and they were just … and I wondered why he didn't – I had being a missionary on my mind. I thought maybe that was where God was leading me, to become a Missionary – but he kept passing by the large flowers and he took me to the very back end of the garden where there were just little flowers on the ground and they were so beautiful ... all colors and this is where the man said to me "This is where I want you. Do you see these little flowers? They are blooming with all their might and that's what I want you to do, wherever you are, don't look for nobody's pulpit, the world is your pulpit you just tell the world about me and I'm Jesus". So that's what people began hearing, about Jesus. My friends had wondered what had come over me because now I was always talking about the Bible to my coworkers, I was always talking about the Bible. At lunch time, instead of going to the lunch room, I would find a corner and sit and read the Bible because I knew I had to take God's Word to the people like He said so that's what I did and I'm convinced now that is my calling because when I meet somebody, the first thing I'm going to find out about them is if they know Jesus and would they like to know Jesus and tell them what I know about Him. I always keep a Bible with me because the Bible tells me not to lean to my own understanding so I know if I can't lean to it I can't tell you to lean to my understanding so I always quote scripture.

Me: What do you think the attraction is with you and young women that are in your life? You have so many that are always calling, visiting, taking you out to dinner, plays or wherever and they are just drawn to you... what do you think that is about?

Mother: Sometimes they need to know what makes me tick. What is it that keeps me going and that's been happening for a long time. They want to know why I didn't attend some movie or go to these different things and I'd tell them I had to be studying the Bible and sometimes I would think I wasn't going to have any friends but then they'd come back for more so my friends gravitated from that. I didn't know it was going to do all of that but I thank God that since He told me to help His people that He sends me people to help. So, these women need advice and I give them advice the best that I can and I pray for them and pray with them and take up time to talk with them so the circle just grew.

There is never a dull moment. I remember one time you spent a little time at my house, stayed with me for a short time and the phone rang anytime through the night (Me interjecting "All through the night, chuckling) because I tell them if they need prayer or advice from the Bible to call me because sometimes people can't wait until tomorrow they need help right now. I have had people call me about to commit suicide and they need to talk now, they can't wait until tomorrow so I have always told them "call me!" Of course, my husband had to put up with that. God did bless me, after divorcing my first husband, several years later God blessed me with a good husband and a good marriage and he put up with all of my Christianity and all of the ladies calling the house through the night and visiting because they wanted to learn and thank God he understood that was my calling. I didn't wait to go to Church, I had Church at home and Church on the phone and that is my ministry now. I spend more time on the telephone than I do anything else telling people about Jesus and I love it! I love doing that. Now sometimes they don't like the advice that I give them but I let them know the Bible tells me not to lean to my understanding so I can't ask them to do something that the Bible speaks against.

Me: Did you have any idea that you would have this type of impact on so many people?

Mother: No. It's a surprise. A surprise and a blessing. It keeps me happy. Somebody wants to know about Jesus and I love Jesus and He is ALL - Everything to me, so I just love it. I answer my telephone, it rings all through the night and you used to ask me "what are all these people calling all times of the night?" Sometimes they can't wait until tomorrow, they need help now.

Me: You mentioned earlier that when you Minister to the Ladies you always refer to scripture and you always carry your Bible so that you don't lean to your own understanding and you have your Bible here with you now and I see that it is open, looks like to a certain passage, is there a particular scripture that you'd like to share or leave with us on today?

Mother: Yeah, how I got healed from – you know I had to learn how to love Jesus, I didn't understand that… I struggled, off and on with that for a long time – how to love a God that "took" my Mother but I got healed from that by reading scripture and I would like to share a couple of verses that helped me get healed. When I found the Gospel of John, that was my favorite and still is my favorite book of the Bible because to me, John took me right up face to face with Jesus and he said "behold the lamb of God which takes away the sins of the world and Jesus said if you love me keep my commandment and so I keep the Bible with me because I read it and it helps me to get over my hurt and Jesus said *(John 6:37–44)* no man cometh unto me except the Father draw him and I say whosoever cometh unto me I will in no wise cast out" so I asked my Grandmother one time, did that mean me too? And she said "everything in that Book is for you either to be or not to be. Everything in that book is for you. So then I knew that – He said that whosoever cometh unto me I shall in no wise cast out and that was my healing and I received Christ wholeheartedly and I learned how to love Him and He filled me with His Holy Spirit and that's what keeps me going through the loss of my children, the loss of my husband, the loss of family members which I stood at many graves. Like I said I am the seventh of nine siblings and I stood at their open graves to see them be put away and my father and mother of course I was only six when she passed and all my siblings are gone, I am the only one left. All the cousins and aunts and uncles that I was raised up with after coming to live with my grandmother and then I was raised with the people that my mother knew and that knew her so that is what healed me, the Bible. It's what keeps me going because no matter what happens I trust God. No matter what is going on in my life, I turn to God and He is always there. And I knew that God had called me to take His Word to the people and I wanted to stand out at different places and pass out tracts or talk to people, I guess be a street evangelist and you asked me during that time "Grandmama you think that God is calling you to be a street preacher?" because I was talking about it so much and I knew that whatever I was going to do I needed to be licensed for it cause I didn't want to get locked up so after I met, like you said I used to attend Pastor Bronner's conferences downtown at Motels and hotels you went with me to a few of those so I just fell in love with him and his ministry and so I talked with him one time (after becoming a member of the Church) about wanting to be ordained and he said "Sure I will ordain you" and it surprised me so and he set a time and I said "before all the people? (in amazement) and he said sure I see Ministry in you and so he did, he Ordained me to do what God called me to do. So I thank God for Word of Faith. I had left Beulah Baptist Church and started attending a small Ministry called "The Living Word Assembly" Pastored by Prince and Frances Martin and I loved it for the season that I was called to be there and then God called me to Word of Faith. I had in mind going to World Changers Church… that is what I had set out to do and when I attempted to do that He let me know that in no uncertain terms that is not what He wanted and then He wouldn't let me go to another Church that I thought I wanted to join either. So when I heard from Mrs. Gibson who is Dorothy Cobb's mother (the mother of first lady Nina Bronner) that Dale was going to start a Church, I excitedly asked her where?! Now, my oldest son Jim was married to Dorothy Cobb's sister Inez, and that's how I got to know that family so well. Mrs. Gibson didn't know where the Church was going to be but I asked her to keep me informed and she did and so the first Sunday that he started Word of Faith on Ben Hill Road I was there! But I didn't join that Sunday because I had other obligations to clear up and once I did that I joined Word of Faith and I have been happy there ever since.

Me: I certainly remember accompanying you to that service as well. We have to wrap up the interview. I'd like to thank you Grandmother for agreeing to participate in this interview. I definitely learned a lot and the generations to come will also learn a lot about you and I think this is a very important interview that we've had today and I want to thank you for giving me this opportunity to ask you some questions today about your life and just sharing with us about your life and what a wonderful life it's been and we are blessed to have you and we love you so very much.

Mother: Thank you for taking the time out to do it and Pastor Boyd thank you so much for all that you do for me at Word of Faith. I mean just looking at Pastor Boyd ministers to me.

Me: Praise God. Amen.

Special thanks to Stephanie Burton, who was the facilitator for our StoryCorps interview and to Daniel Horowitz Garcia who assisted me in obtaining a copy of the CD so that I could transcribe it for you to read. For more information about preserving your family history, please visit www.storycorps.org.

Pastor Boyd with us at The Atlanta History Center for StoryCorps interview.

Natural Born *Leader*

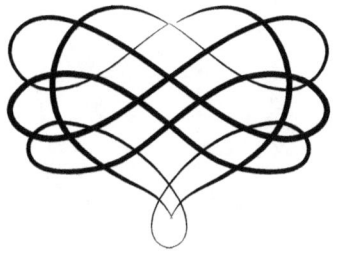

Chapter 3
A Woman of Integrity

Mamama's first real job was with Scripto Manufacturing Co. in Atlanta, GA. She was so glad to come to Atlanta from Winter Haven, FL, by way of a short time spent in Cusper, Georgia, where she lived temporarily with her Cousin Louisiana and her husband Bennie. Then, to only be here for a few months before being hired on with Scripto was like a dream come true!

I told you Mamama likes to GO, right? Well, she went to a "Farewell" party for someone named Stella who was moving to Atlanta. She didn't know Stella before the night of the party. They struck up a conversation and Stella asked Mamama did she want to move to Atlanta. Well, of course she wanted to move to Atlanta!

Stella knew of a family in Atlanta that was looking for a live-in sitter. The family's name was Posey and they had a beautiful house off Cascade Road in Atlanta. Grandma had to leave her three children with her Aunt Florence in Omaha, GA, who she had helped care for her Cousin Louisiana in her younger days. Aunt Florence agreed to keep my mama and uncles until Mamama could get settled and on her feet.

Mamama bonded really well with the Posey family but she knew she didn't want to do domestic work for an extended period of time. She had a friend named Susie who had moved to Atlanta, but she didn't know where Susie lived. Fortunately, she knew how to get in touch with Susie's dad by mail and she wrote him a note asking for Susie's information. Much to her delight, he responded immediately to her request and provided her with Susie's address and phone number.

Mamama and Susie connected with each other. Susie shared that she had a friend named Ruth who worked for Scripto. Scripto was known for hiring people (mostly Black women, at a low wage) through their employee referrals. They would provide the employees with applications to give to their friends to fill out and for Scripto to review. Susie took Mamama to meet Ruth to get an application. She filled it out and Ruth took it to work. They hired Mamama two weeks after they interviewed her. She had to leave the Posey's and everyone was sad.

Leaving the Posey's meant that now Mamama needed a place to live so Susie helped her get a room near Grant Park. Then after a few weeks of working on her new job, she was able to send for her children. Aunt Florence sent Mamama's Cousin Eugenia to Atlanta with the children. This was great because Eugenia was able to sit with the children for a couple of months while Mamama worked. God blessed Mamama with a lot of overtime hours, so she was able to get a larger room for herself and the kids. She had to put Eugenia back on the bus though, because Eugenia was enjoying city life just a little too much (smile).

After Eugenia left, God placed Ms. Mary in her life at the rooming house, to watch the children, while she worked. Mamama was an excellent worker. She was smart, well-spoken, hardworking, cordial and professional. The managers loved her. Every time there was a layoff in the department that she was working in, the managers would manage to skip over her name or move her somewhere else so she wouldn't be affected.

Mamama has always been a woman of integrity – doing what's right because it's right. She's an advocate and a voice for the people. She is not afraid to speak up and out about what's right and what's wrong. These character traits, I'm sure, are what led her to join the Union. I take so much pride in recalling her career at Scripto as a Union worker because she was a steward in the Union. In 1972, she became President of the Union Local #754.

Chapter 4
Always Learning

Mamama has five bookcases in her home all filled with biblical study materials that she has actually read. She has taken many courses and received many certifications in her adult life. She did not receive a college degree but her common sense and love for learning has taken her a long way.

Before she served as president of the local union at Scripto, she served in other capacities that required that she study for the position. As steward, she had to read and understand contracts, learn how to run a meeting in an organized fashion and make decisions that were best for the workers.

In late 1964 and early 1965, Scripto Pen Company faced a major labor strike, in which Dr. Martin Luther King, Jr. participated along with the Southern Christian Leadership Conference. The president of the company at the time of the strike, James V. Carmichael, negotiated with the International Chemical Workers Union, Local 754, to resolve the strike and reach a settlement.

Mrs. Emma Rowland presented scholarship certificates for Scripto and Ferst employees. Beverly will use hers at Georgia State...Cherry will go to Georgia College, Milledgeville.

Mrs. Emma Rowland, a 12-year employee, presented scholarship certificates as chairman of the Scholarship Fund Committee

Chapter 5
Faith

Mamama grew up with the Bible as her primary learning tool for reading. She had many verses memorized and lived the Word to the best of her ability. She had fellowshipped at many churches in her adult life and heard some really great sermons, yet something was missing.

At the time, she didn't know what it was that was missing. She just felt in her spirit that there was more to God than the sermons being preached. God placed in her a hunger and a thirst for His Word so strong that she started taking correspondence classes in Biblical Studies. She attended weeknight bible studies at various churches in the city at the recommendation of coworkers and friends.

Eventually, she found that what she was hungering and thirsting for was the Holy Spirit. She was hungry and thirsty for the unadulterated Word being taught from Genesis to Revelation with "Life application". During the time that I was attending college in Athens in 1981, Mamama attended services at places where you actually had to take your Bible and they read scripture and taught on it. When I came home for visits, I would of course join her on some of these bible studies and, of course I didn't like it one bit. It was nothing at all like what I was used to and these new preachers did a lot more talking making the services ended pretty late.

On one trip home, she invited me to join her at a home Bible Study held by husband and wife teachers. It was held in their living room and I remember that her good friend Sara Robbins (Taylor at the time) was there. It was very different – I had never heard a woman teach bible study and they sang songs I didn't know and they spoke in different tongues (oh my, what was this Grandma had us partaking in?) Although it was different, I kept going with her and listening to what was being taught. I wasn't the warmest and most excited to be there visitor they had ever had by any means, but they always smiled, and hugged on me and acknowledged me every single time that I went.

The ministry outgrew their living room pretty quickly and they moved into a building on Washington Rd. Sometimes, I would be so aggravated to be there that I would sit in the car in the parking lot before deciding to go in. Sometimes a member would come outside to minister to me and encourage me to come inside.

I came to love this small ministry and all of its members. The Living Word Assembly is where I received salvation. It is where I learned to study the Bible and apply the Word of God to my life. I can recall a very difficult time (of many) that I was going through and it involved forgiving someone. I didn't care how much Pastor Prince shared scripture on why it was to my benefit to forgive the other person, I had settled in my mind I wasn't going to do it. Every week, Pastor Prince taught on forgiveness. It became a series. I listened intently and week after week I got a little closer to deciding to forgive this person who had wronged me. One day the Holy Spirit broke through the hardness in my heart and decided that I could and I would forgive this person after all. Pastor Prince announced that he had now been released to move on from that series! God was waiting on me to receive this valuable lesson on forgiveness! It is one I have never forgotten. Now, it is easy for me forgive. In fact, I set my will to forgive anyone for anything they do to me and that's a settled issue. God is good.

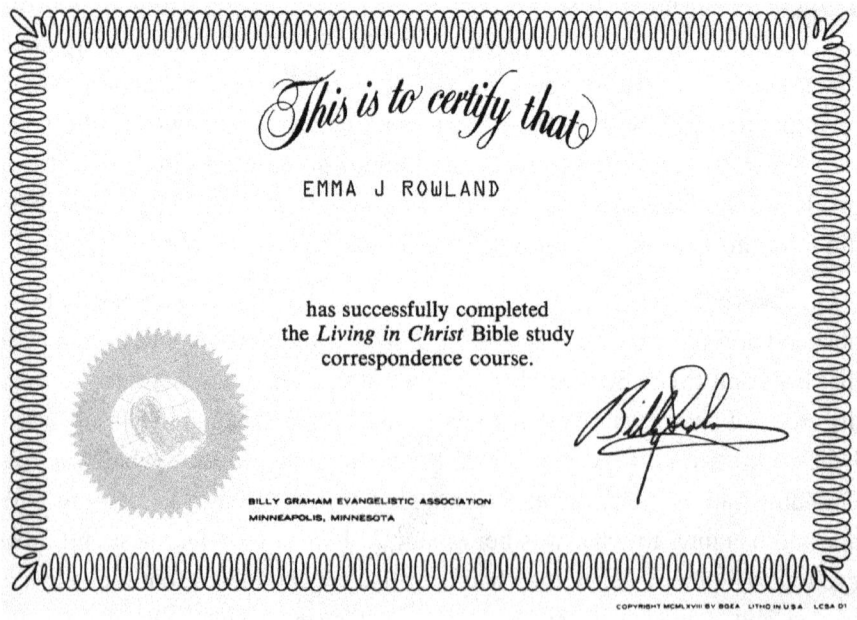

Tribute to Our Mother

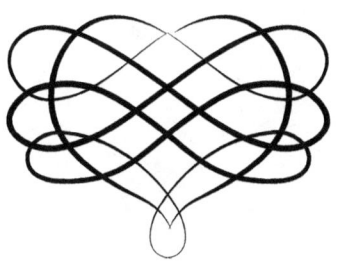

Tribute to Mother

When God told me to write this book about my Grandmother, I knew a biography is not what He wanted me to write. Mamama is way too private to share all the struggles she has experienced in her life. Not only that, I only had 3 months to get this written and you can't do a 98 year biography in three months!

My assignment was to honor Mamama while she is here to read it. So many people have been blessed by her life and have had the privilege of spending time with her and gleaning from her vast knowledge and wisdom. Not only are these people special to her, but she is special to them. Because of the instructions I received from the Father, they have been given an opportunity to share with her and the readers what she means to them.

I have been so uplifted by reading these tributes that I can only imagine what her reaction will be to what she will read on the next several pages. I learned so much about my grandmother and the impact she's had on so many people. I feel that not only will her generation be blessed to read how much she means to so many, but also the generations of each contributing writer will know what an impact she made on their loved ones.

She has met people across many walks of life. They all call her "Mother". I invite you to enjoy what they have to share about their experience with Mother Rowland.

Her Children Rise up and Call her Blessed.

Family

Family Testimonials

In Order to Keep Going, You Have to Keep Going

Once again, we celebrate the life and legacy of Mrs. Emma J. Rowland. This time it is her 99th Birthday, thank you Jesus.

My mother gave birth to three children, two sons and one very sweet daughter. Growing up, my mother lived a godly life before us; she made sure we were saved and baptized at an early age. Mama kept us in church. Every Sunday she made sure we were in church for Sunday School, eleven a.m. service, three p.m. service, back at six o'clock for BTU (later named BYPU), and back again for seven o'clock for night service. My brothers said when they got grown they were never going back to church anymore and they pretty much stuck with that although they would go for special occasions such as Mother's Day; when Mama was honored as the Mother of the Year and other special times.

When we were young children, someone gave Mama a dog for us, (we never said we wanted a dog). After having to bathe the dog one time, we took that dog off and tried to lose him and he kept coming back! After three attempts, though, we were finally successful! No more dog.

Mama raised us with the help of God to be good strong children. She didn't believe in sparing the rod, so we weren't spoiled children.

Mama would take us to the FOX Theater once a year when she was on vacation. That was a really special treat and even though it was segregated at the time, we enjoyed our time with our mama at the movies.

I think that a good relationship between a mother and her daughter is a very precious thing and my mother and I have always had a very good relationship. We have not always agreed with each other, but our relationship has always remained strong.

When you mention the name Mother to me, what comes to mind is kindness, understanding, love, forgiveness, honesty and courage. My mother has taught me all of that and more – she has taught me to be a strong Woman of God. My mother is a precious jewel and I thank God for her long life. Not only is she my mother, she is also my friend and in the absence of my father, she was our father and since the death of my brothers, my brother also.

I know my Mama has been kept here by God for a special reason. My mother has a wonderful, beautiful spirit.

I thank you Mama for always loving me and encouraging me to be the best woman that I can be. I thank you for being a good example for us – your family and everyone who comes in contact with you - to follow.

I thank God for her Word of Faith family. She loves you very much and so do I.

Bishop Dale and Dr. Nina, she loves you two beyond words. Thank you very, very, very much. You have shown her in many ways that you love her dearly.

Mama, you are everything you are because God loves you, and so do we. We will continue to be satisfied with long life, and to quote Bishop Bronner, "In order to keep going, you have to keep going".

Happy 99th Birthday Mama, I love you very much.

Your loving daughter,
Vera

Those Pancakes Though!

I love my grandmother's pancakes! Every Friday, I would get picked up by my grandparent's and a lot of times we would go to Greenbriar Mall because my grandmother loved to shop! Some Fridays, it would be just the two of us and we would go to the fabric store–first Cloth World and then Hancock Fabrics because she could never find what she was looking for in just one store. I didn't mind though I would look through the pattern books at all the pretty dresses and suits. She taught me

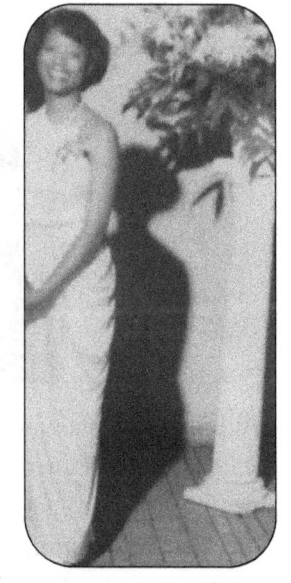

how to know what fabrics worked best with each pattern and how to determine how many yards she needed based on the size or fabric design. She couldn't wait to get home to start cutting out her patterns which she taught and trusted me to do sometimes. She had electric scissors that I loved to use, although she was afraid I would accidently cut myself. She taught me how to pin the patterns to the fabric and baste the fabric to the patterns. I didn't realize how much I had actually learned from her until I started sewing as a hobby. I never wanted to sew clothes for myself because there was a lot of work involved. She always made nice clothes for herself and she even made my prom dress.

But about those pancakes though! My granddaddy wasn't going to let me have pancakes every Saturday - but breakfast at my grandmama's, actually any meal at my grandmama's was a treat because she could sho'nuff cook – and can still to this day. The pancakes were thin AND fluffy! How do you get thin, crispy around the edges and fluffy? I've been practicing for years but my grandmama would turn that black cast iron skillet up on high and somehow they did not burn. I used to say, when I thought I knew how to cook a little bit, I would say, "Grandma that fire is up too high". She would look at it and that was about it. LOL, then she would proceed to cooking as usual. Any meal cooked by Grandma is a treat and every one of them is my favorite. It takes my mama to rave about her fried chicken wings! She may tell y'all about that in her chapter.

When my daughters visit with her, she doesn't have to ask them what they want for breakfast. Pancakes, bacon and eggs is the only thing they want her to cook for them.

Growing up, visits to my Grandmother's house with my cousins Joel, Tyrone and Francine was always a fun time! I was raised an only child so every chance I got to be around my cousins was a joyful time. They were so full of fun and laughter. They all laughed all the time. My cousin Tyrone though, was the jokester. He would aggravate me to no end. He knew how possessive I was of Mamama and he would demand her attention for himself - Grandma Rowland this and Grandma Rowland that. He would never get full! In those days, we didn't go out to restaurants to eat! Grandma would be in that hot kitchen over that hot stove cooking away. Tyrone would always be the first to finish eating and sending his plate back for refills.

While Grandma would be inside cooking, we would be outside with G.P. He kept us entertained by having us help pick fruit off the trees if they were ripe and by allowing the boys to play with his BB guns. I remember one time, that aggravating Tyrone chased me around the yard pretending like he was going to shoot me with that BB gun and everyone thought it was funny but me. Grandma couldn't help me because she was inside cooking.

She loved her gospel music! She had a floor model console record player and plenty of albums. I loved going over to their house after Church for dinner! While she was in the kitchen, I would play the role of "DJ". What you wanna hear Mamama? James Cleveland? OK! Oh my goodness, we played the life out of James Cleveland. He was her absolutely favorite gospel artist of all times. She had records by Shirley Ceasar and several other popular artists but, if you let James Cleveland play all day long she would be satisfied.

It seemed like it took forever for dinner to get ready! I would be starving and these were the days long before microwaves. It really wasn't that much of a hurry because we couldn't eat until my granddaddy got home from church anyway. He was a Trustee at St. Paul AME Church and he had to count the money. I felt like that church must have collected a whole lot of money because he always got home hours after we did. I would stand in that window and watch for his car to come up that hill and I would exclaim G.P. is home!! Now we can eat!

She is so secretive. Or should I say discreet! If you have shared something in confidence to her, you can best believe she has only shared it with God. When I got older and on my own, Grandmama would call me and tell me she cooked but she would not tell me what she cooked! It didn't matter though because whatever it was, I knew I would enjoy it. Then she got to a point where she would cook and wouldn't tell me. Now that made me mad.

As she has gotten older, I can't help but marvel at how feisty she is, how alert, strong and independent she still is. Her walk has slowed down a lot but she is still in her right mind! I don't think that's the norm for most 98 year olds. She's the only one I know at that age so I say we raise the bar so that it is the new norm. I want to be just like her when I turn 98!

Love,
Cheryl

Woman of Steel. Woman of Wisdom. Woman of Faith.

"The woman who gives everyone a little piece of her, not asking for anything in return"

Emma Jane Rowland. My great-grandmother. What a blessing it is to have such a woman in my life. Woman of Steel ... Woman of Wisdom ... Woman of Faith ... But most importantly, Woman of God. Without her, I would not be alive. Not just literally, but I feel like our hearts are intertwined. I have always said to myself that if she dies before me, a piece of me would die too. With that being said, Emma Jane is my rock, my love, my everything and she means the whole world to me. There is nothing I would not do for her.

From what I remember and have heard, she was a major part of my lively childhood. My sister and I spent many of our infant days and summers with her. Almost every time was a new adventure. Mamama, what we call her - the name my Mom came up with as a little one, is most known for her infamous pancakes which she makes from scratch. My sister and I woke up with the anticipation of her delicious pancakes every single morning. It became the main reason why we wanted to come over; we deeply enjoyed those pancakes. Still, to this day, I cannot refer you to a place where better pancakes are served.

Not only did we enjoy the pancakes, but our car rides to the post office, grocery stores, Malls and to McDonald's were very fun and memorable. She would always drive in the far right lane at approximately 40-50mph. Many good laughs and even complaints came from experiencing her slow driving. She would respond with something like "we're gonna get there" or "ya'll shut up and let me drive." I remember it like it was yesterday. That fresh Cadillac smell still lingers under my nose. Sweetest woman ever, so loving and caring. The infamous back rubs, nose pinches, anointments with Olive Oil, the games of "BOO!" Even the painful pinches and use of switches for our misconduct are memorable and appreciated. I will forever cherish those moments.

The saying "Grandmas know everything" is so true. They know what is real no matter how many times we lie or try to hide. Luckily, I can confide in Mamama, so I do not have to lie about anything. I remember back when

I was a freshman in high school, I revealed to her something that I kept a secret from the rest of my family, even my sister. I do not remember why I told her or how the conversation began, but she made me feel comfortable enough to tell her. When I told her my secret, the first thing she told me to do was "Go get the Bible". For the remainder of the night, we read scriptures and she held me until we fell asleep. This is one of the most memorable and essential moments we ever had. It changed my life; 1) because it encouraged me to read the Bible more and seek God first when I am struggling with something, and; 2) because it showed me that if I confide in someone I trusted, maybe they would accept me for who I am. She refers to the Bible for everything and being a woman of God, she is a constant praying woman.

It is truly a blessing to have praying grandmothers in my life. I feel like even if I strayed away from God, even for a small amount of time, I would always be protected because I know that my grandmothers are praying hard. Sometimes when my evening plans are cancelled and I later find out that something bad happened where I was intending on going, I know it was my grandmothers prayers that kept me safe and in the house where I needed to be.

One thing I find interesting about me and Emma's relationship is that we share the same zodiac sign, Libra. I know she, as well as most Christians do not believe in astrology, but I read on it a lot and find it very interesting. Being that we are the same sign, we have similar characteristics and mannerisms. I am able to understand a lot of her disposition and habits more than others. It is not just because we are family, but we are interconnected by our zodiac sign. She is my confidant without me even having to tell her anything because I think that she can sense when things are not going well. It may seem weird, but we understand each other without having to talk about it. When she is around, I can sense her moods and can tell what she is thinking which may not be astrology related, but I do observe her a lot. What annoys and bothers other people does not affect me in that way. My mom commends me on how patient I am with her. Sometimes when she is heavily on my mind, she calls me and vice versa. I know it happens to other people, but I know what we have is special. I have not talked to her about these observations and our interconnectedness, but I do not think it is one-sided.

Ever since my freshmen year of college, Mamama would always try to contribute financially as much as she could. I told her I was fine, but you know grandmas do not want to hear that; they're going do it anyway. She would also write me letters and often send me little thoughtful cards. I really appreciate those. In these letters were Bible scriptures to read, reminders to pray and trust God, and of course those precious "I love you's".

One of my favorite letters reads:

Jan. 27, 2014

Dearest Calina,

I hope you're having a great day, and classes are going well, and friends are faithful. I'm glad you're looking wonderful, and remembering what you're there for. Spend quality time studying and don't forget to pray much! Read your Bible. Make time for it. Are you keeping warm and eating right? Remember, I love you more than you know. Whatever I can do to help please let me know! Have you prayed, smiled and remembered who you are today? If not, stop and do it now. You are SPECIAL and don't you forget it. Let's pray, "Father God in the name of Jesus, guide Calina (me) in everything that she does today and at all times. Keep her safe and saved." I love you girl. Look in the mirror and give me a big smile.

Love,
Mamama

And best believe I found a mirror and gave her a big smile. This letter, along with all the others, definitely put a huge smile on my face. Her handwriting, me reading them in her cute little voice, are the little things that keep me happy and motivated. During my sophomore year of college, I made a promise to her that I would call her at least once a week. And I have held that promise for the most part. She loves my phone calls whether we talk for 5 minutes or 45 seconds; she just wants to hear my voice. Sometimes just hearing her voice turns a bad day into a good one. She is such a sweet and gentle person. How could you not love her?

As you can see, she plays a huge role in my faith. Every single time that I see her or talk to her, she tells me to pray, pray, pray. She stressed the importance in reading the Bible and making time for God. Something I am truly grateful for. Not only does she play a role in my spirituality, but she plays the biggest role in my future meaning my career path. I am an aspiring geriatrician and health care giver for the elderly population. Spending time with her has strengthened my patience with the elderly and has allowed me to be able to familiarize myself with elderly mannerisms and behavioral trends. Considering the fact that she made huge impacts in others' lives as well, my family and I are contemplating opening up an Adult Day Care/Elderly Fitness facility named after her. I want her name to be remembered and her legacy to be upheld in the best way.

A fascinating thing about growing up is that you learn to connect with people on different levels the older you get. I am glad that she was able to watch me grow through several stages of my life and be there for me as a young adult. She was always precious to me but now that I'm old enough to understand our special relationship, she means a lot more to me. When I tell people how old she is, they always tell me that I am blessed and honestly blessed is an understatement. Words cannot express how much love and appreciation I have for Emma. All of my friends, even the ones who never met her, love and adore her. She is just special and will forever hold a special place in my heart. She often tells me not to break her heart and I will carry out that request for the rest of my life.

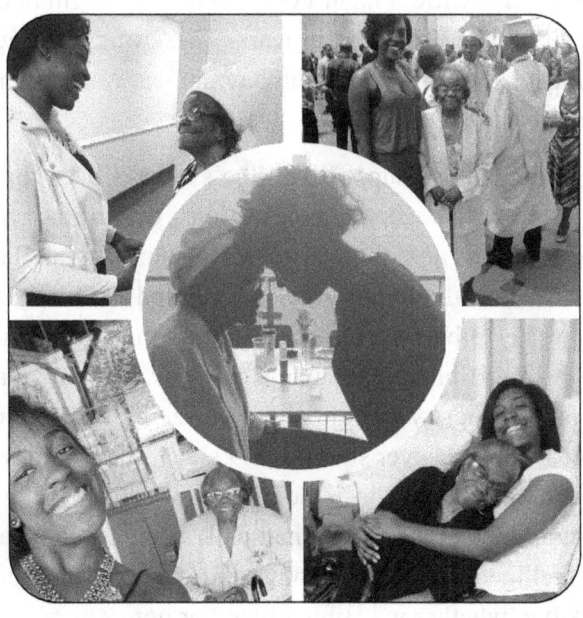

My name is not 'Distian' it's 'Distian'!

Where do I even begin to talk about how much I am blessed to have a great-grandmother? An independent, strong, praying, fried chicken making great-grandmother. To everyone else she is Mother Rowland, but to me, she is Mamama–a name given to her by my mom when she was a child.

I can remember when my sister and I would spend weekends at Mamama's house. Those were very happy times. She had a huge bed, cable tv with all the channels. Most importantly, we knew that anytime we spent the night, that meant that we would be having her famous buttermilk pancakes in the morning! These weren't just any regular pancakes. She would cook them to perfection. Even now at 98, they still taste the same - delicious!

I believe that it's important to think about all the little things that make someone who they are today. Especially when dealing with someone as special as Mamama, it's important to try to remember every experience and time that you've spent with her. I can remember a particular time I was out riding with her in her silver Cadillac Deville and she was driving with her knees! It was the coolest thing ever and I guess her way of showing me she wasn't old just yet. The older I get, the more I appreciate and value the fact that she is still present in my life. Seeing her at my graduation was literally the best moment of my life. I hadn't cried that entire night but as soon as I saw her cute little face, I erupted in tears. These of course, were tears of joy because I just know how important that moment was for her and I know how proud of me she was.

She's so genuine and so supportive. She's always been there for every awards program, every academic celebration - everything! She's always there to pray for me and to talk to me when I'm in the mood for conversation. She's truly an amazing woman and definitely a woman of God. She knows her Bible cover to cover. I don't think there's anything she loves more than the Bible and the name of Jesus. Anytime that we would spend the night with her, we would always sleep in the bed with her and I can remember - that whenever she couldn't sleep, she would wake up, turn the lamp on, and immediately open the Bible. It was like clockwork. Almost every few hours, she would just automatically wake up and read the Bible. She's a very intelligent woman and knows the answer to just about anything you could ask her, whether it's Bible related or not.

I also love how independent she is. I can remember her never wanting to use a walker and God forbid - someone asked if she wanted a wheelchair. The most she's ever needed was her cane and honestly, I still don't think she really needs that. The fact that she's able to live on her own is truly the works of God. She can still read and write and see and hear just fine (sometimes). Oh and her memory is impeccable! She always tells the story of when I was probably 2 or 3 years old and couldn't say my name correctly, but would try to correct other people on how to say it. She always tells me that I used to say, "My name is not 'Distian' it's 'Distian'!" My name is Christian by the way. Of course now I can properly say my name, but still she loves to tell that story just about every time we're all together. I still love to hear it every time.

She is truly blessed and anyone who comes in contact with her can feel and sense that.

I am very proud to call Emma Jane mine. She's my Mamama and I'm her "Distian".

For those that know

Emma Rowland or better yet, Grandma Rowland and I came to know one another in a very precarious way. My first impression of Grandma Rowland is of her driving up to Vera's house in her Cadillac wearing her "Sunday go to meeting" hat. When they told me her age, my mouth fell open.

For me to speak of Grandma Rowland, I first must tell you about the person that introduced me to Grandma Rowland. This lady strives EVERY day to be exactly like her mother, Grandma Rowland. Vera Pope adopted me as her nephew and in turn the whole family embraced me, so please forgive me if I talk about Vera in tandem with Grandma Rowland. TO me they are one in the same. While they are different in some ways, they share a Love for GOD, family and people. For those that know, you would agree.

I met Grandma Rowland and Vera when I was literally at a transition in my life. My life was in total disarray. Marital strife, financial woes and the list goes on and on. The world was beating me down so bad until I thought my name was Drum. To put it bluntly, I was walking backwards. I had lost my mother shortly before; one of my grandmothers was stricken with Alzheimer's and the other was aging fast. In step Grandma Rowland and Vera.

The very worst thing that can happen to a person, especially a man, is to lose self-confidence. It is the Ultimate fear for someone who has been in control ALL his life. Unbeknownst to Grandma Rowland, she re-instilled all of the confidence of old. From time to time, I would perform chores around Grandma Rowland's house. The whole time I'd be working, she would shower me with praise; "Lord, thank you for sending me such a smart grandson", "Look at Grandma's handsome boy", "I love my Grandson". grandma Rowland singlehandedly built up my sense of self-worth. Vera, on the other hand keeps me humble. She constantly scolds me for being late and not always doing what I said I would do.

They both gave me a remedial lesson in manners. When we go places, I have to RUN to open the doors for them. They let me know they are QUEENS and they expect to be treated as such. All the things I learned as a child, I have to display while with these two. I may not always practice being a gentleman with others but it is mandatory with Grandma Rowland and Vera.

I can go on and on talking about ALL that Grandma Rowland and Vera "loved" into me. I would be doing everyone a disservice if I failed to mention that they taught me to trust in the Lord. Grandma Rowland is a living embodiment of God's promise. It's one thing to hear religious rhetoric but it's another to actually see and touch a real life testament of the power of walking with Christ. Grandma Rowland has been blessed with longevity, Good Health and Sound Mind. She has been blessed with three children, two of which she has  survived. She has been blessed to have grands and great-grands, not only to have them but to have the mind to know them. Grandma Rowland is a true woman of GOD!

I am going to end this by saying that like most children, once Grandmomma has shepherd us through the storm, I have become negligent in my duties as a child. My visits to Grandma Rowland's house have become less frequent. The intervals between visits growing longer and longer. But like the Prodigal Son, I know my way home. So, when I was asked to write "something" about Grandma Rowland, I considered it an honor and a privilege. The whole time I have been putting my thoughts to paper, I have had to wipe away the tears. I think about all the kind words and motherly gestures when they were in much need and all too far in between. I am so happy to give Grandma Rowland these flowers (praise) while she is still here to smell (hear) them. I owe her a debt I can never repay!

So, for those who know …

Emma Rowland is EVERYTHING we should hope to be. A person to be cherished and commended. I love, love, love my Grandma Rowland!

Reginald M. Sapp
I AM

Thoughts of Grandma Emma

Any new venture can hold uncertainties, fears, excitement and can even produce a bundle of frayed nerves. Joining a new family (when you are not a newborn baby), can cause a person to experience so many emotions.

And so it was, when I was introduced as Marc's wife over forty-five years ago.

I was brought to Atlanta for the purpose of meeting the patriarch and atriarch of the "family".

Already feeling self-conscious when I realized my dress was a wee bit short, my nerves began to shatter. After introductions were made, a silence crept into the room. I was waiting to see who would be the first to speak. Not me! While Mr. Rowland (G.P.) just stared, Grandma Emma broke the silence. She began talking, which calmed my nerves and allowed me to feel more at ease. Her voice has always had a calming effect. My thoughts were that they realized I was gainfully employed and was not like the boll weasel looking for a home. I didn't want anyone to think of me as a leech.

After the brief visit, I leaped into Marc's car to reflect on what had just happened. I could not forget the loving face and voice of the woman I had just met.

As time progressed, we made visits to the in-laws and they visited us in return. Grandma Emma was always the perfect hostess, making sure everyone was comfortable. She bestowed kindness, patience and genuine concern for all, especially the outsider.

Learning of her christian beliefs, I have noticed that these reflect her daily practices. Her church has always been a very important institution in her life and her church members have always been family. Grandma Emma has always had a flair for fashion, with shoes and handbag to match every outfit.

Now, when I reflect over the years and how well I have known her, she rates among the best; always being a loving mother, grandmother and wife. She even accepted my child as one of her grandchildren. The two of them shared talks, laughter and she gave advice on whatever he asked. Our youngest son loved her cakes and even looked to her for advice on what to feed his pet rabbit. Perhaps he thought that was a way to get more cake. Most of all, my boys remember her exquisite cooking and her special hugs.

Speaking of cuisine, all of us were so excited to be at her table, especially holidays when the goodies never stopped coming.

Whenever there is a problem, Grandma Emma is always a first responder. I have always been proud to be so close to a real sweetheart and to call her my mother in law. I ask that she continues to pray for me as I for her. May she always be smiled upon by God as she continues to share her love with all of us.

Much Love,
Joyce Rowland

EMMA

Germanic origin meaning:
Whole, Universal, ALL-EMBRACING!

That is what Ms. Emma Rowland personifies.

Ms. Rowland was first introduced to me by her granddaughter, Cheryl Pope Clark in 1985. She EMBRACED myself and my daughters, Traci and Shana Pope, with love, support, encouragement and boundless positive energy. Time spent with Ms. Rowland at her home surrounded by family and friends, feasting on abundant and delectable dinners, was where I had the pleasure of being entertained by her wittiness, spiritual gifts and affection.

Ms. Rowland's existence is contagious as she flaunts her youthful spirit and wardrobe. What a stylist! Always admiring her spunk and sassiness, I remember complimenting her on her "fresh" outfit and she replied, "I don't recall seeing an old folks clothes department in the store!"

Ms. Rowland inspires us all to live life to the fullest, love all, enjoy the fruits of your labor, dress to impress and most of all, keep GOD first.

EMMA...whole, universal...ALL-EMBRACING! Thank you for who and whom you are...One of GOD's Greatest Gifts and THANK YOU for the awesome opportunity to have shared a part of my life with you.

Affectionately,
Denise C. Pope

Cousin Emma Jane

This tribute is to my cousin, a wonderful woman of God.

I have known Cousin Emma Jane most of my life. She was my mothers, Louisiana, first cousin. I remember her visits to us in Forest Park, Georgia. Not only was she a cousin but a dear friend to my mother. They were like sisters. My mother always talked about her visits and looked forward to the next one.

She has always been, as far as I can remember, a very mild mannered even-tempered woman. Later in my adult life, I became her hairdresser for many years. My cousin has always been and will always be in my opinion a woman of prayer. She has been my spiritual prayer partner. I call her, even now, to have her touch, and agree with me on many different situations.

In summary, I can truly say she is honorable and loved. I thank God for having her here in my life and being a Godly woman. I can only pray that her example of Love and Grace is passed on for future generations - inside and outside of our family.

Elder Minnie Taylor

Happy 99 Years of Caring and Sharing
WITH LOVING THOUGHTS AND MEMORIES OF "MY" COUSIN EMMA JANE

Cousin Emma Jane,

You have and always will hold a "special place" in my heart. Traits of your warmth, compassion, gentleness, caring and God-Like Kindred Spirit are etched in my brain.

Your words of wisdom are, too, etched in every cell of my being. My love for you are beyond words!

On a closing note... YOUR SWEET POTATO PIES ARE OUT OF THIS WORLD!

God's Perpetual Love and Blessings are upon you!

In Gratitude to God for Blessing our Family with your Radiance.

Annie Mae Stublefield

Cousin Emma (an example for us all)

Even before my father, Robert Lee Carter (sixth child and third son to Webster and Florence Morten Carter), was born, Cousin Emma started her ministry of help, support and obedience by moving to Omaha, Georgia (Stewart County) to be company and help for the first new born daughter to Webster and Florence Carter (Aunt Louisiana). Aunt Louisiana is the oldest sister to my father (Robert Lee).

At birth, Aunt Louisiana was an only girl among boys born from Grandpa Webster's first marriage to (Jessie). So, Cousin Emma was asked / told to go stay with Grandpa Webster and Grandma Florence to be "girl" company for baby Louisiana in Omaha. Her job, as I understood it, was to assist with the care for and play with the young cousin and help Grandma Florence.

One of my favorite stories to hear from Cousin Emma was about a wedding / party that she had looked forward to attending, because there was always cake to be eaten at the after party. Well, as it happened, Cousin Emma could not attend the party because duty called for her to attend to her charge (baby Louisiana). So Cousin Emma did not get her piece of the cake. The look on Cousin Emma's face each time she tells this story makes me believe she still misses that piece of cake.

On one visit, I asked Cousin Emma what words of wisdom would she pass on to us ... her reply was, "read the bible like you are going crazy". After thinking about her reply; how else will you understand that Exodus 20:12 "Honour thy father and thy mother: *(comes with this promise)* that thy days may be long upon the land which the Lord thy God giveth thee. And Joshua 1:8 "This book of the law shall not depart out of thy mouth; but thou shalt meditate therein day and night, that thou mayest observe to do

according to all that is written therein: *(comes with this promise)* for then thou shalt make thy way prosperous, and then thou shalt have good success".

Cousin Emma, whether she knew it or not, while obeying her mother and father some 85 plus years ago, started a lifestyle of obedience that has proven to be a key to longevity, spiritual prosperity and success.

The family of your Cousin Robert Lee Carter loves you and thank God for your sweet spirit and Godly example.

With Love and Respect,
The Family of Cousin Robert Lee Carter, Sr.
(sixth child and third son to Webster and Florence (Morten-Carter))

My mother, Daisy Lee (Carter) Harris, is a first cousin to Emma Jane Rowland. I first met Emma about 15 years ago. Through her, I have met other relatives in the Atlanta area that I didn't know existed. Her warm personality and knowledge of the family history has always impressed me. Even more impressive has been her faith which has helped lead me to a deeper and richer relationship with our Lord. It has truly been a blessing to know and love her.

Curtis and Sherrell Harris

Friends

Friend's Tributes

She is my "Go to"

I have known Mother Rowland since I was thirteen years old (I am now 80). We were neighbors for several years and attended Beulah Baptist Church under the leadership of Juan Burt. Mother Rowland and my mother sang in the choir.

I moved out of the state for thirty years. When I returned to Georgia, I joined Word of Faith Family Worship Cathedral and was oh so happy to see that Mother Rowland was also a member.

I have a dear friend that was very sick in the hospital some years ago. The nurses called a "Code Blue" because he was in cardiopulmonary arrest and very close to death. The doctor said he would not live through the weekend. I called a church member and told her to call Mother Rowland and tell her to pray right now for him. I believe the scripture that states, *"the effectual fervent prayer of a righteous man availeth much"*. That was eight years ago and my friend is alive today and doing fine. I feel in my heart that was because Mother Rowland prayed for him.

When I need spiritual advice or any other direction, Mother Rowland is my "go to". I love her so much. It brings joy and happiness to me whenever I'm in her presence.

With loads of sincere love,
Gloria G.(Gault) Buchanan

P.S. I agree with her daughter Vera who states ... "I have never known mother to be worldly".

Wisdom and Truth, Without Compromise

My journey with mother Rowland started as a young lady re-locating from Flint, Michigan looking for a fresh new start in life. In my mind, Atlanta was all that I needed, to be complete. I was looking for a change from small town living, and wanted the excitement of a big city for the completeness that I long desired. Upon my arrival, I started with the social scene; meeting new people and going to the various parties, football games, and concerts.

My next step upon my arrival in Atlanta was to find a church home. My relationship with God was very important, and I knew that it would be vital to my existence being so young and alone in such a large city. It took about three months of visiting before I found a church home that I knew was for me. It felt so good to be in fellowship again. My father always made sure that my brother and I "never forsake the assembly of the Lord," so going to church had been a staple in my life from an early age. It was strange to me that I had the desire to fellowship without the requirement of my parents, but the seed had been sown.

On one night of my weekly partying with my friends, I went to the club and it did not feel the same. I looked around and it seemed like the same people, same music, same scenarios in every club, every state that I had ever been to. In that moment right there in the club, I looked up and said "Lord there has to be more to life than this," and that is where my real journey began to find the fulfillment that I was looking for in moving to Atlanta. I left the club immediately and never returned to another one ever.

The church that I was attending was a young church from the leadership to the congregants. The transition from the world was minimal. I could not go back to the world, and at the time I thought that the church would be like the Garden of Eden; no strife, no backbiting, no illicit behavior, just the peace and joy forever. Then the reality of the church came to me; these people are just like me, they need help too.

One day I was at work as a hair stylist, and I had gotten to know the sweetest lady, Vera Pope, Mother Rowlands daughter. As I began to express my concerns to her, I had a lot of questions, and I wanted a lot of answers, but she just sat there, and finally she said, "I don't know, but I know someone that does." That is when I met Mother Rowland.

I called her on the phone and her voice was so big: I thought "wow she must be a big lady." As we began to talk, I knew that she would always be a part of my life. She spoke with wisdom and truth without compromise. She said "Resa, Holiness is still right, and without it no man shall see God, and it is not in the church it is in you!" Her words were piercing to me, and they made me accountable for my own relationship with God, not dependent on the minister or distracted by the congregation.

Since the time of our meeting twenty years ago, Mother Rowland has been a mother, mentor, and friend. In the beginning of our relationship, I was able to depend on her to lead and guide me in prayer, then the day came that I was able to pray for myself and watch the Lord move in my life in the same way as when she prayed for me.

I thank God for the influence that Mother Rowland has in my life: it is truly a privilege and an honor, to experience the seeds of holiness that she plants into so many women's lives that come up as the fruit of virtuousness. I love her for helping me to find the true fulfillment that I moved to Atlanta for, it was Jesus.

Clarissa "Resa" Flowers

An Angel walked this way and decided to bless my day.

I have the distinct pleasure of paying homage to a dear friend that is the grandmother of a dear high school friend of mine. I finished Douglass High school in Atlanta and became friends with Cheryl Pope Clark. Thereafter, our lives reconnected by way of our daughters attending Benjamin E. Mays High School in Atlanta. We have had several movie dates, pot luck dinners and a number of other related outings however nothing that we have shared has impacted my life as much as when Cheryl introduced me to her beautiful and wise grandmother, Mrs. Emma Rowland.

I met her as I made a visit to her home in S.W. Atlanta. Mrs. Emma was then 96 and lived alone in a pretty, free standing ranch home that perched high on a hill. As I parked at the bottom of her extended driveway, my mind wondered who could pull this hill every day??? I approached the carport and rang the doorbell and there to my surprise stood a woman, all of 4.5 feet tall, adorning a colorful dress and jewels intact. She greeted me with a solid hug and a very sound "Welcome". She ushered me in and her home was immaculate!

Every nook had its very own story to tell about her walk in this journey called life. There were others in the living room, who were her relatives including Cheryl and her daughters. We had a light lunch and sat around for some good conversation – we all listened intently as she poured in to us stories of old. She spoke about the Lord who is the HEAD of her life and told of her childhood years. She spoke about how she was raised in the COUNTRY and how she and her cousins would walk miles to the market and walk through fields of watermelons. She often bellowed in laughter as she reflected on certain parts of her childhood!!!

All of her stories were filled with knowledge and lessons to learn from, however, not any of the stories she shared made an impact on me as much as when she spoke about the Lord.

I have an 18 year old daughter and a 5 year old son in which I had my son at the ripe age of 47!!! When Mrs. Emma learned of Brandon, my 5 year old son and how I had him at a late age she, pulled me to the side and began to prophesy into my life about what God had implanted in my life through the birth of my son. She told me that he is a BLESSING and that he has a specific PROMISE over his life. She sternly advised that I plant the RIGHT seeds in him and teach him to be a gentleman and walk upright in the admonition of the Lord and how Brandon will bless my life in years to come.

As I would interrupt him as he would reach to touch one of her many figurines and what-nots, she pulled me back and said, "No, let him be a boy, that's what they do!" She sternly said that I should allow him to explore for that's how he'll grow!

MY, MY, MY, But God!!! It was as though God Himself spoke to me at that very moment.

Her words are always so eloquent and in line with the scriptures in the bible. She further began to pray over my life and she petitioned God on my behalf and she asked that God watch over me and my family and provide for us and make a way for us in these perilous times. She even spoke over the life of my daughter, Hope Ashlin, that she would be respectful and mindful of her actions and that she walks with the Lord as her guide and to be a leader and not a follower. Tears flowed from my eyes when this powerful woman of God spoke! My heart raced and my body began to shake as the Holy Spirit made HIS way through her home and through me!

My life has been richly blessed by this powerhouse for God and she is a wonderful testament of God's FAVOR, God's LOVE, God's ACTIONS, God's ANOINTING and God's SPIRIT. Her charisma, Faith walk, health and strength and her sound mind are my personal goals that I wish to experience in my GOLDEN Years.

I salute Mrs. Emma Rowland on this day and in days to come.

My mentor, my adopted grandmother, my Living example of FAITH, My prayer warrior and MY FRIEND!!!

> God Bless you Mother!
>
> Carry ON. Carry ON!!!
>
> WELL DONE!!!

Lovingly, Your adopted family;
Tracey L. Hodges
Hope A. Hodges
Brandon L. Hodges

In Awe of her Love

My fondest memory of Mrs. Rowland was shortly after being released from the hospital after surviving a domestic violence incident. She invited me and my children to her home, along with her granddaughter and my best friend Cheryl, for Thanksgiving dinner. I remember like yesterday, twenty years ago, being awestruck with her love and care for us. She served us like royalty, and she prayed for my continued recovery and stability and blessings for us all.

Thank you Jesus for Grandma Rowland.

Forrestine "Tina" Lewis Hightower

Sixty years or more, My how time has passed. You've been my "other mother" through a friendship that will last.

Jim became my guy, sister Vera and I made friends and Homer became my classmate.

And you, a woman on whom I could depend.

I'll always love you "Mama"

It's you I truly adore

If I could count all the stars in the skies above

I could but love you even more!

Your other daughter,
Katherine "Kitty" Thomas

"God is good. His loving kindness endures forever and His Faithfulness extends to all generations."
Psalm 100:5

Minister Rowland, May your sweet, sweet spirit always dwell among us. May you forever stay busy and don't fuss.

May you continue to move freely as butterfly wings. May your heart be filled with joy of great things.

May your love of God continue in peace. May we always see the fruit of the spirit that you release.

Thanks for being a wonderful inspiration in my life. Happy 99th Birthday!

Love. God Bless.
Queen S. Emory

Neighbor

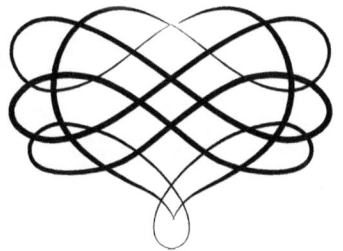

Neighbors Acclaim

Go to the Street Called Straight

Mother Emma Rowland has proved the Bible, God's Word to be true if we live by it, in that you honour your father and mother according to *Exodus 20:12*, "Honour thy father and thy mother: that thy days may be long upon the land which the Lord thy God giveth thee".

Mother Rowland has lived almost five generations. According to *Psalms 90:10*, *"The days of our years are three score years and ten; and if by reason of strength they be four score years."*

God promised us in Psalms 91:16, *"With long life will I satisfy him, and shew him my Salvation."*

It is amazing to me how many years Mother Rowland tried to sell her house and move off of Amber Place. Thank God He did not allow her to move. Her house sits on the highest hill on our street - as a Queen's house, a Prayer Warrior's house, an Intercessor's house should. It is important for her prayers to saturate the air and flow down with the blessed anointing of God's Word to sustain us. We are blessed to have such a model neighbor to live on the hill in our neighborhood.

I tease Mother Rowland that she is like Job; she has some children in Heaven and God restored her to have adopted children like us who will do anything for her at this time in her life.

Mother Rowland is our Naomi. We will glean the fields for her. We are her Ruth according to Ruth 1:16 *"And Ruth said, intreat me not to leave thee, or to return from following after thee, for whither thou goest, I will go: and where thou lodgest, I will lodge; thy people shall be my people, and thy God my God. Where thou diest, will I die, and there will I be buried; the Lord do so to me, and more also, if ought but death part thee and me."*

Just like Naomi, Mother Rowland has taught my sons and daughters and caused them to walk in the ways of the true and living God. We will follow her as she is a plumb line to many of us to line up beside. Mother Rowland has taught us to go to the Street called Straight, according to Acts 9:11a. *"And the Lord said unto him, arise, and go to the street which is called Straight."* (And when we got to Straight Street, we know to turn right – Mother Rowland's GPS system).

Mother Rowland taught us, as she lived in front of us, God's Health laws found in Leviticus and Deuteronomy "fast as well as pray."

> *Father God in the precious Name, Mighty Name of Jesus, I come before your Holy and Righteous Throne to thank you for giving us Mother Rowland. She has been an angel on assignment from You for us. She has proved to us that Your Word is true. She is an example of Proverbs 31:1-31. She is a Virtuous Woman. Her Children and her Children's children and those of us she took under wings have called her blessed. When she speaks, she opens up her mouth with Wisdom, Knowledge and Understanding. Thank you Lord that Mother Rowland has lived almost five generations and has been a Natural Born Leader to all of us who love, adore and admire her. Bless her Lord from the Crown of her head to the sole of her feet. I plead the blood of Jesus over her and all that she does according to Revelations 12:11. In the Name of Jesus Christ of Nazareth we pray. Amen*

Neighbor Lillie Wade
Amber Place

The Help

The Helps Praise

More Than a "Domestic Engineer"

January of 1980 was the beginning of a wonderful love affair and enduring friendship that goes beyond our wildest dreams.

It was a bitter winter day when we moved from our small condo in Stone Mountain to our new house in Atlanta. We were thrilled to be closer to our growing business in Buckhead that, at the time, brought many opportunities and lots of challenges. In order to keep up with an ever-growing business, travel schedule, and a lively social calendar, we came to the conclusion that we had to find someone to help keep our new home in shape … and we knew that person had to be female. When we met Emma a few weeks after moving into our new home, we forgot about the cold rainy days of winter as we were warmed by the glow that our special "Domestic Engineer" radiated at every turn.

Shortly after getting settled in the new house, we met Pat and Charlie Davis, our new next-door neighbors and now long-time friends. Before we met them, we had the impression that we had moved someplace that was out of our league as there was a very large Cadillac parked in front of their house whenever we would make a random run home during the workday. We would soon come to know that the Cadillac belonged to their "Domestic Engineer", Emma, and the Davis' drove a Ford station wagon!!! We just knew we had to meet this lady and get her to work with us, too!! We LOVE ladies with class and pizzazz and Emma surely possesses both!

Ultimately, charming Emma came to our house for an "interview". We were so nervous that she wouldn't like the house, or us because we already fell in love with just the thought of her. (Who wouldn't want a shiny big Cadillac parked in front of their house, if only for a once-a-week decoration!!)

She looked the house over carefully and wasn't a bit shy about what she would take on and what she expected in return. We joked with her that it was just the two of us with no kids except our beloved Siamese cat, "Snooks". We felt it was very important that Emma and Snooks got along well. That was a deal breaker for us and indeed Snooks loved her (and he didn't care for many people). We think that Emma came to love Snooks as much as we do.

It didn't take long before it was clear to us that we had been blessed by having not only someone to help us with household chores, but we had gained a new family member, as well. And that's exactly the relationship that developed between us. Emma was the perfect addition to our family. She proved that she was reliable, honest, trustworthy, hardworking, loving and proud of her accomplishments.

Every once in a while one of us would come home from work in the middle of the day and found that she loved listening to her transistor radio on her Gospel station while she worked. We suggested that she might want to use our stereo to play her music and we took some time to show her how to work it and tune in her station. The next time one of us came home during the day she was still listening to her music on her little radio and we asked why she didn't use the stereo. She said she liked moving the transistor radio with her from room to room, hanging it on a door knob by the thin strap of its case, to keep her company. We never saw the need to bridge the subject again.

After a few years, we asked Emma if she would like to help us entertain at various parties we hosted at home. With her typical undaunted attitude, she said that she'd be delighted provided we show her the ropes and train her. For more years than we can count, Emma was the first person guests encountered when arriving at our parties. Her warm smile is contagious and she was the person who instantly made our friends feel at home and welcomed. Many times we would hire a catering service for special events, and while they would bring their own "crews" we put Emma in charge of making sure the outside help marched to her same tune. She was a brilliant leader in that regard. And while she was the first person guests interacted with upon their arrival, she was also the last to say goodbye to them; on certain occasions, people would search the house to say goodnight and thank you to Emma for making their stay in our home so enjoyable before leaving.

We remember, with glee, the night of our annual Christmas party when we caught Emma in the kitchen speaking in a low voice with our friend

Monty Collins and others. Wondering what was going on, Manny gave Monty an inquisitive look and Monty said, "Manny and Don, you cannot let Emma retire. How can you have a party without Emma?!!"

Emma had been talking about retiring from us and the others in our neighborhood and we knew that day would come sooner than later, but at the time we just weren't ready to lose her. We think that Monty's message resonated loudly with Emma since, before leaving for the night, she pledged us to secrecy from the neighbors that she would continue on with us and go into "semi-retirement" by coming to only us once a week. Of course the neighbors saw her car in front of our house every Wednesday for many years thereafter. So much for the big retirement secret!

Emma was always "Emma" until we attended her 90th birthday celebration at Word of Faith Family Worship Cathedral. It was a Sunday we'll never forget as we truly had an epiphany!! We discovered that she is "Mother Rowland" and is held in very high esteem by the hundreds of friends and church members who came to celebrate her life. We loved seeing her in the sanctuary singing and swaying and praising the Lord that she loves. We will never forget that moment. Her joy was infectious and obviously, her council as a church elder is very much sought after and revered. As much as we loved her before, we now had even more respect for this dynamo of a lady and the deep spirituality she exemplifies and shares with so many.

2007 was a bittersweet year as Emma at age 91 decided it was time to pass the "Domestic Engineer" baton to someone else. We couldn't bear the thought of having someone other than Emma in our house. We were so afraid that we would lose contact with her and that she would drift out of our lives. We couldn't imagine coming home on a Wednesday without finding a lovely hand written note left by Emma, telling us how much she relished being in our home and what a wonderful day she had enjoyed.

We tried taking care of business and the house, too, and we found it difficult to alter our schedules to step into Emma's shoes. Our hearts ached for her but we managed to keep in touch and would invite her for lunch at a restaurant now and then. She may have been gone but she has never been forgotten. We manage to stay in touch with her on holidays and throughout the year and just hearing her voice on the phone brings joy to our hearts and is always uplifting.

After living without Emma for a couple of months, we figured out that we were just not cut out for domestic chores. So one day we asked her if she would give some thought as to a recommendation for her replacement. She said "let me give this some thought". Not long thereafter, she informed us that she had a candidate for her replacement and we invited both of them to our home for a meeting. Mother Rowland introduced us to her good friend and fellow church member Marilyn Wright. Again, we didn't know how life would ever be the same without Emma; but with Emma's mentorship and helpful hints and advice, Marilyn stepped into her new role with eagerness and the same values that we immediately recognized as Emma's. We think that Marilyn might have had fair warning from Emma that being chosen for the job wasn't to be taken lightly. Emma was a bit stern with Marilyn and told her in great detail what SHE expected from her if she accepted the job as our new "Domestic Engineer". It didn't take long for us to realize that Emma had made a good choice and that Marilyn would make her proud. It tickled us when we would chat with Mother Rowland and she would always ask how Marilyn was doing, as if she was checking up that we were satisfied with her service. Marilyn has been with us for nearly 7 years and is a tribute to Mother Rowland. We adore Marilyn and are thrilled Emma brought her into our lives, too.

We look forward to our frequent chats with Emma who never ceases to amaze us with her energy and zeal for life. We were determined to keep her close to us when she retired and our admiration for her will never wane. Clearly she has enriched us and we praise the day she came into our home and our lives. God Bless You Emma! We love you and love being part of YOUR family.

Don & Manny
Don Vellek and
Manny Beauregard

IMPACT

It is not often that you come in contact with someone that makes an impact on your life. Emma Rowland did just that for our family. Emma provided a valued service and friendship at a time when needed by our family. She always presented a positive spirit regardless of any challenges she was facing at the time. We were and are truly blessed to have Emma for a friend. We especially enjoyed the element of surprise when she showed up one week driving one of her new Cadillacs!

This photo of our son Brent with Emma clearly shows the admiration he has for her!

Pat and Charlie Davis

Faith

Faith Testimonies

Beulah Baptist Church
Pastor Emeritus W.L. Cottrell, Sr.

Please receive my expressions of gratitude for having known and served with your darling grandmother, The Reverend Emma J. Rowland for many years. She was one of the most dedicated servants at Beulah I have ever known. The Beulah Church has been on the cutting edge for change for many years. I salute her calling and all of you who are so abundantly blessed through her ministry. I take courage to know that after 125 years, Beulah's present Pastor is a woman; Pastor Trina Evans.

MOTHER OF THE YEAR

The Beulah family honors Mrs. Emma J. Rowland as our Mother of the year 1959.

We feel that it could not have happened to a more devoted person. She has expressed this devotion in the height of her ideals, depth of her conviction, and width of her endurance.

Thus, we join in with Luke in saying,

"Hail thou that art highly favoured, the Lord is with thee: Blessed art thou among women."

Expressions of Love

When I received the email from Cheryl in reference to her accepting the call to write a book about her grandmother, Reverend Emma Jane Rowland, I started giving thanks to God, and the first thing that came to my mind was what a mighty God we serve! As I continued to read the email and it read you are invited to be a contributing writer because you are an important part of her life, I praised God even the more for Cheryl being so open and unselfish to allow others to be a part of such a beautiful occasion. God's divine connection, purpose and plans for our lives are so phenomenal; He confirms His word with signs and confirmations. What a timely honor!

Just last November, while working on a Georgia history project, the class had been charged to speak with someone who might have experienced some of the earlier happenings of Georgia's history. I called Mother to get some information from her in reference to some of the things that she remembered about Georgia history. At this time, she shared many incidents and life experiences that she encountered during the "Jim Crow" era. After listening and documenting her encounters; through the tears, my remarks to her was thanks so much for sharing. However, our conversation did not end there. I told her she needed to write a book; her words to me were "baby, I cannot, there are too many tears". I said to her, I do understand, but I believe that someone should do this. Before we ended our call as usual we prayed.

I didn't know that God was dealing with Cheryl, her granddaughter, so when I got the email from Cheryl, in reference to how the Holy Spirit had been dealing with her about this challenge, again, all I could say was thank you God! I was happy, and grateful. Another thing wonderful about this project is that so many people who lives have been touched by Mother Rowland, will be able to share their expressions of love, and experiences that they have witnessed with and through her life.

For me, I can truly say that she has touched my life in such a rich and rewarding way. I will share just a few ways in which she has touched my life and how we came to know each other. In 1971, I had the honor of meeting, as I affectionately call her, "Mother" Emma J. Rowland. She was my sons', Cameron Taylor, Sunday school teacher at Beulah Baptist Church, 170 Griffin Street. At this time, I only knew her as a young, vibrant, smiling, sassy, classy, caring, dedicated, humble servant in the church, and in the community. She had so many of the characteristics that my mother had; therefore, I had a desire to get to know her in a personal way. Little did I know that she was watching me singing and glorifying God - desiring to know me as well. However, at this time both of our lives seemed to have been going in different directions. We were both busy taking care of our families and serving in different capacities in the church; therefore our paths did not directly cross at this time in our lives.

As God would have it, in 1979, I became a part of another ministry; I thought to myself, well that is it for getting to know Mrs. Emma J. Rowland. God knew the purpose and plan He had for our lives, and He also, knew the desires of our hearts. He knew that we both had the desire to get to know each other personally. Being the loving God He is, in 1981, two years after my being affiliated with another ministry, our paths crossed again. Both of our prayers had been answered. We ended up serving God together within the same ministry and really getting to know each other spiritually as well as close up and personal.

Not only did we serve within the same ministry, but we became as a family. We often would eat at each other's home, and fellowship. She began to call me her daughter; therefore, Vera, who is her biological daughter, and I began to call each other sister; Cheryl, her granddaughter calls me aunt; I really feel close as a family. We have prayed together, eaten many meals together, cried together, laughed together, shared the Word of God together, and to this very day; we are still enjoying our wonderful, God ordained relationship.

I feel very honored and blessed to have known Mother Emma Rowland for over 40 years and we remain close until this day. She is my mentor, Mother in Christ, and a very special friend whom I love very much, and I believe the sentiments are the same on her behalf as well as Vera and Cheryl.

Sara Robbins

Love in Action Counts

Mother Emma Rowland - wrapped in nothing but *joy, joy, joy*.

For God so loved me that He knew that I would need a Mother Emma Rowland in my life. A Mother Rowland who, without "fan-fare", moved in and around the Church of my childhood (Beulah Baptist Church, 170 Griffin Street, Atlanta, Georgia) actively engaged with a warm and quiet spirit that caused one to notice her movement unintentionally. Her movement inspired, encouraged, empowered (although I didn't know these words then), and modeled what it meant to be a dutiful and faithful servant.

As I look back over my life (60 plus now), I am sure, without any doubt in my mind or reservation in my heart, that the Mother Rowland that "touched" my life in such a special way then, is still demonstrating that only "love in action" counts.

Finally, the vision of her smile is etched in my memory as coming from way down deep. To the end that it was just as contagious, as it was generous. It always seemed to say, "I'm here and I care".

I remain grateful for her love and support and it is with these sweet and precious memories that I am compelled to lead by example as she did and engage in ministry with a *"Mother Rowland steadfastness"* which is wrapped in nothing but *joy, joy, joy*.

Thank You Mother Rowland and Happy Birthday!

Gloria Weaver
August 2015

Birthday Blessings

It has been years since I have seen Mrs. Rowland; however, I have had the blessing of speaking to her recently. From my memories, Mrs. Rowland has not changed. She is still the sweet, gentle, loving woman that I knew as a child!

I grew up in Beulah Baptist Church with Mrs. Rowland. I thought that she was a beautiful, well-dressed woman who had a special love for people ... especially children.

I remember her kindness and her love for God. In all my years at Beulah with her, I only heard words of love, and Glory to God!

Happy Birthday Mrs. Rowland!

Zelma Leandrew Harris
Daughter of Deacon Andrew and Deaconess Zelma Harris
Granddaughter of Deacon Arthur and Deaconess Clara Harris

Stand for Jesus

Emma Rowland has always had a special place in her heart for me, and I a special place for her. It has been an Honor and

a Privilege to know her for 43 years of my life. I love what she stands for: JESUS ...

Cameron Taylor

I would call Mother Rowland from time to time and she talked so strongly for her age. I would always pray for her while we were on the phone. She would reply back, "Thank you man of God, I really appreciate that". And sometimes she would pray for me.

Brother Jerome Ragsdale

Full of God's Amazing Grace

When I think of Mother Rowland there are many things that come to mind. One of which, is grace. She is so full of God's amazing grace. The other would be wisdom. To be in her presence you are ever learning and being enlightened. Mother Rowland is such an awesome blessing and such a great testament of God's amazing and unmerited favor. From the time I met Mother Rowland, as a young child until now, she has been a tremendous blessing in my life. I am so fortunate and blessed beyond measure to be graced with her presence every other week to care for her hair. I absolutely love, adore and wouldn't trade it for the world the time that is spent with her.

There are no words that describe my love and gratitude that the Lord saw fit to place this amazing, phenomenal, awesome, wonderful, beautiful being of a person by the name of mother Emma Rowland in my life! I praise God for her. She is the epitome of beauty, grace and wisdom. She is loving and kind. She always has a kind and gentle word to say. She brings an instant smile to my face when I see her, because my thought is – look at grace and beauty walking live and in the flesh.

What more can I say but I love her with every fiber of my being! Thank you Cheryl for affording me this opportunity to be apart of something of this magnitude. I love my momma Rowland to pieces!

Thesa Taylor Long

The Living Word Assembly

Dr. Prince Martin, Jr. and Dr. Frances Martin, Pastors

"Who can find virtuous woman?
For her price is far above rubies"
Proverbs 31:10 KJV

–MOTHER EMMA ROWLAND–

To God be all Glory and Honor. Mother Rowland is a Mother of Mothers. She is one who flows with love, joy and the peace of God. She is one who loves much and all others seem to respond to her, in love, also.

When we met Mother Rowland, she would come and be in attendance in our worship services held in our home at that time. Then, as still now, she showed the love of God in her life. She demonstrated knowledge and great love for the Word of God.

It was in 1982, that she was one of the first twenty people who joined our ministry-The Living Word Assembly. When our ministry moved into our church building located on what was known as Tell Road; she became the teacher of our Sunday school adult class. This was a very popular class for our adult church members. Everyone seemed to love her teachings. She taught with great knowledge and love for the Bible and much love for God's people. God really blessed her, and she had a very successful class.

We remember how our children also loved Mother Rowland. She always had in her purse all kinds of candy goodies and treats. The children would gather around her for treats. She loved the children and they too, loved her. She truly is a mother of mothers.

"Therefore being justified by faith,
we have Peace with God
through our Lord Jesus Christ"
Romans 5:1 KJV

Let's Talk About Her Beliefs

A woman of grace, and a woman of great wisdom, and we affectionately call her, Mother Rowland. She has demonstrated to all who know her that she believes in God, the Father, God the Son, and God the Holy Ghost. She believes that "God so loved the world that He gave His only begotten Son, that whosoever believes in Him should not perish, but have everlasting life." Her belief in the Trinity is deeply rooted in her heart. She embraces His Word in totality. She believes that when you hold on to His unchanging Word, and never let go, that all grace will abound toward you. She believes that Calvary said it all. She believes that because of Calvary, we are free to walk in Victory. She believes that Jesus took our place, and took all our sorrows. She also believes that Jesus will return for His Church and we will forever be with the Lord.

Her life influences and draws people to believe in Christ. For he that wins souls is wise. And through wisdom and great love, she reaches out to everyone demonstrating the kingdom principles. She believes that there is hope for everyone. So, she lifts the name of Jesus over all of her problems, and people are drawn to believe in God. Mother Rowland is a Kingdom builder. Through her still, soft spoken voice, she is able to communicate, touching the soul and minds of people causing them to believe. Praise God for Mother Rowland's life of none wavering faith.

> *"For God so loved the world,*
> *that he gave his only Begotten Son,*
> *that whosoever believeth in him should not perish,*
> *but have everlasting life."*
> John 3:16 KJV

Let's Talk About Her Faith

Mother Rowland's faith is strong. She is rooted and grounded in faith. For without faith, it is impossible to please God. Her faith in God ignores darkness and causes her to stay focused on Jesus, the author and finisher of her faith. Her faith in Jesus is the dominate force that has propelled her success in life. And irrespective of all the circumstances she has faced, her faith has made her whole. She speaks to circumstances, telling them to be removed, in the name of Jesus. Her faith has caused her to be able to stand amidst life's challenges. And because faith is vital, she releases it through prayer, singing and meditation. God honors her faith and the Body of Christ honors it also. She is steadfast, never wavering in unbelief.

Being single or heavenly minded has helped her to bring every stronghold into captivity, exalting the Word, giving no place to darkness. We have been amazed at how she walks in the light. We know that it is because she daily abides in His Word. God's Word is truly a lamp unto her feet and a light unto her path; that is why her faith is, and has made her whole. Praise God!

Her standard of life reveals that there is nothing more important than having faith in God. For faith is the substance of the things hoped for, and it is God's proof of what He says, and what He is able to do. She believes that if people would imitate the faith of the elders in the church, and our forefathers, they too will be overcomers of every weapon formed. Mother Rowland's life of faith demonstrates that the Holy Spirit has illuminated her entire being. And because He leads and guides her, the wisdom of God is always present to heal and to deliver.

So, come on everybody, let's give thanks to God for Mother Rowland's unshakeable faith!

> *"Therefore, being justified by faith,*
> *we have peace with God,*
> *through our Lord Jesus Christ"*
> Romans 5:1 KJV

Let's Talk About Her Lifestyle

Mother Rowland's lifestyle is to be honored, because it demonstrates the character and attributes of the Lord. You can just see the fruit of the Spirit operating through her. And the rewarding thing about walking in His character and attributes is you remain youthful, and also they add longevity to your life. Mother Rowland looks so good. She has not aged at all. She gets around amazingly. This is truly a demonstration of walking with God. Everyday gets sweeter and sweeter.

Mother Rowland's life speaks volume. It shows you how to live abundantly, being fruitful all of your life. She wears an ornament of grace. It is revealed in her mannerism. Her smile and all of her gestures are heavenly. If everyone would simply implement a smile, especially during difficult times, you too, like Mother Rowland, can add longevity to your life. Jesus said, "I have overcome the world." Mother Rowland tapped on to that revelation and her life reveals that she has conquered sickness, and all the works of darkness.

Another amazing attribute that Mother Rowland displays, is peace. We have never seen her upset, dismayed nor in disparity. She has learned to stay focused on Jesus, who gives us peace. And in the time of trouble, she allows the peace of God to rule rather than yielding to darkness. This peace surpasses all understanding. This peace paved the way for becoming more than a conqueror. When Mother Rowland faced one of her biggest challenges, the Holy Spirit quickened," fear not, only let peace rule." So she activated that Word, and we all can clearly see the results.

She also has a lifestyle of trusting in the Lord, excluding her mind, and depending with her whole heart on our infinite God. And because her life relies on the wisdom of God, she always comes out the winner. The kingdom principles that Mother Rowland embraces, disengages her from the kingdom of darkness. She has the amazing ability to yield to the Lord – no matter the circumstance.

Her lifestyle goes back for years. We believe that when Jesus became her Lord, He catapulted her into a new dimension in order to walk in the realm of the spirit where there is righteousness and joy and fullness of life. And this Zoe life that exudes through her is the greatest influence for humanity today.

Mother Rowland, we honor and salute your life in its entirety.

> *"Her children will arise up*
> *and call Her blessed"*
> Proverbs 31:28 KJV

Let's Talk About Her Calling

Mother Rowland has been called by Jesus to minister His Word. With the anointing to teach His uncompromising Word, many have been blessed. She has been faithfully teaching for years. She is a minister who rightly divides the Word, imparting the revelations of Jesus Christ, freeing the souls of people.

Little did she know that teaching the Word would be so rewarding. And even when she accepted the call, changes started immediately. She could see that people were encouraged as they listened to His Word; for it brought life to people, giving them hope. And when you can visibly see changes in the lives of people, it makes your heart glad.

God began to perform His Word. People were healed, and delivered from sickness, poverty and disease. Each day she would abide in His Word and God would give her revelations to meet the needs of His people. She was able to witness the growth in His people. They started to release the flesh and walk in the spirit. She taught them to love God with all their heart, mind, soul and all of their strength. She also taught them to love their neighbor as the Word directed. The amazing thing about love is that it starts in the home. Mother Rowland planted love in her immediate family. Her daughter, Vera, walks in agape love even now. She taught that charity starts in home and then it spreads. Today, agape love is the dominate force that Mother Rowland exemplifies. Loving God is the apex of her faith. And because she loves Him, it has been the foundation of her calling.

Everyone called by God to minister the gospel must sit at the Master's feet and wait for the empowerment of the Holy Spirit before being fruitful. In doing this, all grace will abound toward you. And you will be a light intruding over the kingdom of darkness, setting the captives free.

Mother Rowland's anointing is her assurance of being called by God. She graciously wears this anointing with humility. This anointing sealed her calling to do as the Holy Spirit leads.

Thank God for the anointing on Mother Rowland's life.

> *"Who hath saved us, and called us with and holy calling,*
> *Not according to our works,*
> *But according to his own purpose*
> *And grace"*
> 2 Timothy 1:9

Let's Talk About God's Grace

Mother Rowland will be the first to let you know that all that she has accomplished in life has been by the grace of God. For Jesus, said, "Without me you can do nothing." God's grace is so amazing because it abounds. Yes, it is by grace that we are saved, not of works. So we give God all glory, honor and praise for all that He has done for humanity.

God's grace was sufficient for Mother Rowland in the good times and rough times. His grace brought her through life's ups and downs. And because God is our sufficiency, we cannot fail, for there is no failure in God. He holds us up no matter the circumstances.

Mother Rowland honors God. She always gives to Him all of the glory, honor and praise. She is truly an ambassador for the Lord. She loves His Word as well as sings His praise. She is quick to say, "To God Be the Glory" and "Lord, I Thank You For All That You Have Done."

Her life is saturated with glory, honor and praise for Jesus, God's Son. Her every breath is to praise the Lord. For He and He alone has done marvelous things. He has proven that He would never leave her nor forsake her. She held on to her profession of faith, and God's grace was with her and brought her through every situation.

Her life is a banner of truth, displaying righteousness, rendering unto God all glory, honor and praise.

So, Mother Rowland, we bless you and celebrate your life, for truly God's grace has been and is sufficient for you, delivering you from every circumstance because of your love for Jesus Christ.

With Honor and Much Respect,
Dr. Prince Martin, Jr. and Dr. Frances Martin
Pastors
The Living Word Assembly

> *"Let us come boldly before the throne Of grace*
> *that we may obtain mercy*
> *And find grace to help in the time of need"*
> Hebrews 4:16 KJV

A Smile Goes a Long Way

It was 1985 and my mom and I had just joined the Living Word Assembly. I was a teenager at the time and living a Christ-life was so new and confusing to me. My mom came home one day and told me that Mother Rowland was going to host Friday night bible studies in her home for the young ladies at the church. That announcement made me nervous. I had seen the seriousness of Mother Rowland's love of God and was a bit intimidated. Would she have me learn every scripture in the Bible? Would I have to recite Psalm 119 in its entirety?

The drive to Mother Rowland's home for the first bible study was nerve-wrecking at best. After knocking on the door, the woman on the other side of that door greeted me with a warm and loving hug. She smiled at me and had the most beautiful expression of love in her eyes. She had prepared snacks for us and asked that I help myself to them. "Wow!" I thought, "She is so nice!"

We all took our places on her cozy sofa and the Bible study began. She started with prayer and then began reading scripture. She went around the room, asking each of us what the passages meant to us. We had such a great time just learning about God from a woman who wasn't intimidating, but who simply loved God and shared her wisdom and love with us. Needless to say, I couldn't wait for the next Friday night session.

Those Friday nights have undoubtedly made an indelible impression on me. Because of Mother Rowland, I learned that God was real and that He will speak to us and will intervene when there are problems. I learned what it meant to serve and love God. I learned how to conduct myself as a young woman. I learned that a smile goes a long way when Jesus is in the heart of the person who delivers it. I learned to love Mother Rowland as much as she loves me.

Crystal Walker-Banks

Mother Rowland,

God has blessed you with wisdom from above. He has given you knowledge and we have all seen it in your expressions of love for everyone.

I was inspired by stories of your encounters with the Lord. How He opened your eyes, let you see truth, and gave you the victory.

I also remember how you took the young girls under your wings and taught them God's love.

Thank God for You!

Love,
Sister Doris Davis
(Crystal Walker-Banks mother)

Loving her Forever

I would like to thank God for allowing me to honor one of the most important women in my life, Ma Rowland. My Great-grandma passed when I turned 20yrs old. I never thought I could love, care and cherish anyone as much as I did my Great-grandma. Oh but God. He saw fit to put her kindred spirit in my life. I call her Ma Rowland. It was through much prayer and stern talking, well let me say, her gentle way of letting me know she meant everything she was saying, that I am who I am today.

She has played a major part in helping to develop me into the woman I have become. Words cannot express what she truly means and always will mean to me. Loving her forever.

THANKS MAMA IF I NEVER TOLD YOU BEFORE, KNOW YOU ARE APPRECIATED!!!!

Sherry LaVonda Johnson –Molden

Moma Emma Rowland

I thank God for the day Moma Emma Rowland came into my life. That was the beginning of a beautiful, nurturing, lifelong relationship, ordained by God, Himself. At that time I was a young, single mother with three young children. We had moved to Atlanta, the big city, away from all of our family, relatives, friends and everything that was familiar.

The Lord led me to The Living Word Assembly World Evangelism Church where I found Moma Emma Rowland. There, she was the Adult Sunday School Teacher. Each Sunday morning she would profoundly teach the "Word of God" with enthusiasm, zeal and simplicity. I received from those teachings the foundation needed to raise my family as a "Godly Woman". She encouraged her students to pray, read our bibles, believe the Word and do the Word of God. Her teachings were the example of the Godly lifestyle she taught about and lived.

I remember the times when we (The Adult Sunday School Class) were invited, along with other members from our church, to Moma's home for dinner on Sundays after church. The meals were always delectable, plenteous, cooked with love, served with Southern hospitality and would please any palate. I looked forward to going to the house that sat on a steep hill, filled with love. I had not mastered that driveway, so I would park on the street. Thank you Moma Rowland for those "good times".

When I first met Moma Rowland, I suffered greatly from asthma. I was hospitalized because of this condition just about every weekend – the devil was trying to prevent me from coming to church. Moma Rowland said to me one day, "Mencia, the Lord told me to fast for you, to turn my plate over for you".

She did and God honored that fast. Praise God! She was one of the Saints God used to help me receive my healing. I am eternally grateful to her for her selflessly fasting for me. I called her a few years ago to reiterate my gratitude.

The genuine love that Moma Rowland gave to me and my children she now shares with my grandchildren. They have come to know and love her as well.

THE BEST IS YET TO COME, MOMA ROWLAND!!

Love Always,
Mencia Johnson

A Woman of Faith
Rev. Emma J. Rowland

"Your appreciation is a wonderful thing. It makes what is excellent in others belong to us as well." Voltaire

When the words "Respect and Admired" comes to mind, Mother Emma Rowland comes immediately to the forefront.

No words can express, no act of gratitude can relay, no gift can represent what your love and support has meant to me. I extend my heartfelt appreciation for everything you are. You have been my mentor/teacher and have been with me on my spiritual walk for many years. You won my award for "most admired" person in my book.

Mother Rowland, you are one of the most genuine, compassionate, soft spoken, faithful and downright decent person I have ever met in my life. From the moment we met, over 35 years ago at The Living Word Assembly, I knew we would be divinely yoked together. I was drawn to you and the God you worshipped.

Being the only one saved in my family at that time, I desperately needed a Naomi in my life and God sent you. Your life was a powerful witness to the reality of God. You became my Spiritual Mother that loved and cared for me. What a profound impact your life made! I bless you for always being there to cheer and to guide me on this journey of life. We have cried and laughed so much that now when I reflect on God's goodness and how He brought me through, you come to mind.

Your life and ministry inspire me and others to press on in Christ Jesus. Thank you for being one of those people that just make others feel good. When I am in your presence, the warmth that is received is like you are sipping on "a cup of comfort" that warms your heart, lifts your spirit, and enriches your life.

Over the years, you have been like a blanket of comfort during some of the darkest and scariest hours of my life. There were many occasions in my life when the goings were tough, and I got bumped and bruised by the circumstances of life, but your ultimate comfort encouraged me to see God's grace in the midst of difficult circumstances. I'm grateful for you being so supportive, and assuring me that I would come through it. It made all the difference! However, I always considered it a little strange that during some of the darkest times in our lives, we were both going through at the same time. Nevertheless, I witnessed God's miracle healing in your life and it ignited me to trust God as well.

I will always cherish the visits, phone calls, notes of encouragement and times of fellowships. I believe the characteristic that makes you shine is your ability to build relationships with your students on a personal level. It is most evident when you receive testimonies and thank you wishes from students who have been touched by you in some way. They always refer to you as one of their favorite teachers. We all have that "teacher" that we look back on fondly and remember him or her as the teacher who directly influenced us in a memorable way and you are the one! You taught me to teach!

Perhaps one of my favorite things about you Mother is your great sense of humor - the funny saying or comments you make that tend to catch people off guard. One piece of advice you gave me is: "you have to know when to leave the party." From time to time in the midst of situations, I stop and think of you with a smile!

I am thankful that a woman of your abilities will spend your days in the classroom teaching your many God-daughters to be Christ-like and an

example of what a person who turns her life completely over to the Holy Spirit for guidance looks like. Your love and support will always be remembered in good times, and as encouragement in bad.

Today, we say thank you for always inspiring this generation with a positive, life-changing message with teachings for all ages. It is amazing how many young people greet you every Sunday and you encourage them to never stop praising and serving the Lord. It never surprised me because you always had a voice that was bigger than yourself, and always wanted to use it for something larger than yourself.

Mother, you are a rare individual who leaves your imprint on the lives of others. It is my great pleasure and privilege to call you a truly outstanding mentor and a dear friend. I am indeed honored to know someone who has done so much in teaching and ministering, and whose capacity for learning and teaching shows no signs of slowing down.

Mother is like a well ... she creates a thrust and atmosphere that you just keep coming back for more. Thank you for adding love, wisdom and laughter to my life!

I love you Mother!

Lillian Gray

Mother Emma Rowland: Spiritual Icon!

I am honored to call Emma Rowland "my" Mother Rowland. That's the way she made my entire family feel, whenever we were in her presence. She is known to my wife Marva, my son Jordan and myself as a spiritual icon. Mother Rowland stood among the greatest people we have ever known in our lives. I have a beautiful natural mother in my life but mother Rowland was our spiritual mom.

We called her an icon because of the way she led a spiritual before us. Mother Rowland was a spirit-filled pioneer and trail blazer in our gospel community. Her love for Jesus was contagious. She really showed us what it was like to live a spirt-filled life and made us want to commit to a deeper walk with the Lord.

I remember when we first met mother Rowland. It was at an informal bible study at a church we were thinking about joining (The Living Word Assembly). I was a brand new Christian and so was my wife. I had so many questions about my faith and the faith community we had chosen. I loved the format of this church's Bible study. It was like really being in class. The pastor just did not teach the Word, but he also asked questions during his lesson. Mother Rowland responded to one of the open- ended questions the pastor asked the Bible Study class. The pastor asked, "What have you done for the Lord lately?" Mother responded to that question with such simple but powerful insight. Mother talked about how our agendas sometimes do not add up to be anything when we measure it against what is God's plan for our lives. She shared her testimony about being "busy" all day doing "the right thing but not the God thing" and not accomplishing one thing for the Lord. I was unsure about joining that local body of Christ, but after her response, I knew what congregation God was sending us to join.

Sometimes, I think about where I am today and ask myself, what if Mother Rowland had not have been in Bible Study that evening or what if she did not respond to the question the way she did? It would have made a drastic turn in my life and I would have not joined the church the Lord had intended for my growth. I am who I am today because of joining that congregation. It was then that I knew she was going to have a major impact on our lives. Fortunately, we were not the only family Mother Rowland had this kind of an impact on. The whole congregation called her Mother Rowland and benefited from her love and wisdom.

As we continued to fellowship at that local body, her love and kindness drew us even closer to Christ through her. Mother was always there for my family, providing Godly love, prayers, and so many good times in the Lord. My family continued to grow in Christ because of a "little four and a half feet tall" strong black woman we call Mother Rowland, our spiritual icon.

Truly Honored to Call her Mother Rowland,
Willie, Marva, and Jordan Edwards

A Proverbs 31 Woman!

On or about January of 1991, Sara Robbins invited me to go to church with her, at The Living Word Assembly; there I met Mother Emma Rowland, (my God gift and loving mom). We bonded instantly.

Mother always sat on the left side of the church, front row. I started sitting next to her and laying my head on her shoulder. We started interacting by calling each other. Visiting, celebrating various events, spending quality time together.

I became part of a prayer team she was on at the home of the Late Sister Hattie Hewlett's home. We became very attached to each other. During my early years knowing her, even though I was strong in the Lord and the power of His might, she was reinforcement and support for me.

Years ago my ex-spouse kicked me and my son out. A friend of mine "Muslim" took us in and I paid her half of all the expenses. One time, she went on vacation to the country of Panama and did not pay the light bill before she left. I lived in darkness for one whole month, because she took my part of the money for her trip to Panama. Every night, Mother and I would talk on the phone, until I got sleepy; she made herself available for 30 days. She prayed with me each night, encouraged and exhorted me. Above all she loved on me.

Mother is a woman full of wisdom, she is the righteousness of God, and she reinforces, encourages and supports any and every one she comes in contact with. She is a loving confidante and a woman of excellence. In my heart I see Mother as a rock and a woman of power. A Proverbs 31 Woman!

A friend and a mother, that sticks closer than a brother; a woman that confesses the word and speaks truth always. My spouse Fernando and my son love her and call her mother too!

I must say aside from Jesus in my life, she is my #1 BEST FRIEND and I love her very much and she loves me too!

Ms. Emma Rowland is a Godly woman you can talk to about any subject, she is slow to speak and wise! Wise!

She is a God given vessel and I celebrate and honor her!

Mirna Oglivie

I Knew God Brought us Together

One of the few people that I know who understands and accepts others with real love, her wisdom and compassion with truth is so awesome. Because of her wisdom from God, motherly love, unbelievable understanding, patience and never judging, I have learned from her to share God's truth with love without judging and being patient with others. I never thought I could be used of God to counsel with anyone but now that I find myself doing just that, I also find myself using her methods: first of all making others feel loved gets their attention to listen to the truth that is sometimes hard to hear because knowing this person of God loves you - it has to be truth.

To share God's Truth, I learned from her that you've got to be strong and stand alone a lot of the times because the devil will always send someone along to pick at you. We have had some good laughs at some really dumb things the devil has brought to us.

I love it when I'd say something about being normal and she'd say, "What is normal?" For reasons some may not understand, I loved it because I knew she really got it - the understanding of life itself.

I am a much better Christian because of knowing her and our being a part of each other's lives … seeing how she lives and applies God's Word to her life - not just talk. I knew God brought us together the moment I saw her pull up into the church parking lot and our eyes met as I was sitting in my car waiting for the doors of the church to open on my first visit. I knew she was indeed a true woman of God.

Cheryl, I could write a book on her because of all she means to me but… I won't. This is your book. This is such a wonderful thing you are doing for her. I also thank you and your mom for sharing her with so many people… especially me because of the impact she's had on my life that is being passed down to others through me, to so many others which, in turn, will continue to be passed down … what a legacy!

Much love in Jesus,
Jerri Sullivan

Mother Rowland and Me

I remember Mother Rowland's feasts. Boy, could she cook! She would lay out a Sunday spread—I'm talking four or five meats, all of them exquisitely seasoned (yummy) and more delicious side dishes than you can imagine to go along with them. Then there were the breads and, yes, awesome desserts. She could really lay out an awesome spread.

At one of Mother's Sunday feasts, I recall Mother talking about the sin in the world. She said, "If God doesn't do something about this sinful world, He will owe Sodom and Gomorrah an apology!" We all laughed, but her words were so profound and thought-provoking and true. I've repeated those words to others who found them profound as well, and I've always given Mother Rowland her credit, even to people who don't know her.

I am blessed to know and be loved by Mother Rowland.

Sincerely,
Tracey L. Smith

Word of Faith Family Worship Cathedral

Bishop Dale C. Bronner and Dr. Nina D. Bronner, Pastors

Mother Rowland, as she is affectionately called at Word of Faith Family Worship Cathedral, is a blessing and an inspiration to all who know her. As a charter member, she was one of the first persons to join WOF. In fact, she joined on the very first Sunday that Bishop Bronner (Pastor Bronner at that time) gave an invitation for membership at WOF Family Worship Center (at the time) located at 2435 Ben Hill Road in East Point, Georgia.

Being the awesome woman of God that she is, Mother Rowland wasted no time utilizing her knowledge of God's Word, and her undeniable gift as a teacher. She began to positively impact the lives of countless women, while faithfully serving as a Sunday school teacher and as the ministry leader to Women's Daily Walk Ministry. She has faithfully served in these positions for well over 20 years.

In the early years of WOF, we held a women's retreat in Cottonwood, Alabama, and Mother Rowland was one of our speakers. The Word of God just flowed out of her mouth as she shared with all who were in attendance. I can still remember her message as she spoke in the chapel of Cottonwood Hot Springs Spa and Motel. As she spoke the Word of God with conviction in her soul, I hung onto every word that proceeded out of her mouth as she spoke about building your life on the Rock. What a word!

Mother Rowland is such a graceful, loving, witty, wise, respectable, virtuous woman of God. She allows the Word to dwell in her richly. She is a woman of unshakeable faith in God, and her close relationship with the Lord is evident.

God has truly blessed Mother Rowland with a long, healthy, productive life. When her work on this earth is finished, and it is time for her to go home and be with the Lord, undoubtedly, she will hear the Lord say to her, "Well done, thy good and faithful servant. Enter into the joy of the Lord."

May you be blessed, encouraged and inspired by all that is shared by some of her WOF family.

Dr. Nina Bronner

What About You?

I love Emma Jane Rowland with my whole heart. Just knowing I am away from her hurts. God knows that all we do will work for good to those that have submitted to His will, I have my own opinion about His decisions sometimes. Just joking, I trust God with my all and all. He and He alone is my entire reason for being. There is no one else for me.

I want to thank the family for giving me the honor to spend time with Mother. Vera, my sister, you are so loving and giving of yourself to others, may God continue to bless you. Cheryl, God has blessed you with things that will continue to be revealed for years to come. The entire family has been and is a wonderful blessing in my life.

I have prayed over writing this chapter of *our* lives for a while and pray that whoever reads it will be blessed. I stated *our* lives because we are all connected in more ways than we know or want to admit. Once we have accepted Christ as our personal Savior we should address others like family, siblings in fact.

When I met Reverend Rowland, I was going through a rough time. I did not have a relationship with the Lord. I had attended a play that Reverend Blackshear put on for the church; the invitation was given to come to a regular church service. Well, I went to a service and eventually joined WOFFWC. Life was still difficult but I read the bible and learned that God is for me. Regardless of anything else; I trusted God and read Psalm 56 – it is full of great words of encouragement.

My life, by choice is one of continuously learning. I need to have something to set my mind to. The mind is a terrible thing to waste is not just a cliché; it is biblical to take hold of your thoughts. Those that have read the bible know that Job finally submitted to God because God knows our thoughts *(Job 42:2)*. Another scripture that comes to mind is *(Proverbs 24:9)* which states that it is a sin to have foolish thoughts/plans. We need to guard our thoughts with all diligence.

Well, my story has taken a turn for the good and I can only imagine that Mother is happy that I can speak of God so freely. She taught me that *when*, not if, *when* I put God first I am doing things in order. There are so many things I have and continue to learn from this powerful woman of God. My advice to others is to seek God for someone that can help you along on this journey. (Pray, Pray, and Pray), until you feel comfortable talking to God about anything and everything.

Back to when I noticed Reverend Rowland. She has been teaching Sunday school for a long time. I was seeking a class to attend, while WOF was still in transition after the move to the Cathedral, I stopped in on her class. I can tell you she has such an intense way of teaching God's Word it is penetrating. One question that got to my heart was, "Did you read your lesson?" Well, I learned to always be prepared, especially when you are a Christian.

My first encounter with God concerning Mother Rowland was at 3 am. I woke up thinking about the previous day, which was Sunday. This distinctive woman of God is walking down the hallway, getting hugs; showing love and getting pushed around by people that are too busy to watch where they are walking. How can these church goers be so insensitive? Don't they see her or understand that she is precious and should be treated as such. Why is there not somebody helping her, is that how they show love? Just pondering on these thoughts; there was a small voice that said three little words; what about you?

What about me? I was not aware that I could step up to such a task but after a short internal conversation, I decided to trust God. I prayed all week and waited for Mother Rowland to drive up to the church, the next Sunday. I went to her that Sunday and explained everything. She just was so happy and said thank you for being so kind and doing what God has put on your heart. That Sunday changed my life forever. I have such a heart for God that can be attributed to Mother Rowland.

I don't think of myself as special by any means but God has blessed me with this unique relationship. I have been overwhelmed by all the things I have been exposed to because of Mother Rowland. The ability to see others as God sees them, in the spiritual sense. Humility is a trait that Mother has shown me by example many times. It is a difficult trait to work on but I know it is necessary in this journey. I do my best and pray for the Holy Spirit to help with the difficult parts.

I have gotten to the age that my body does not want to function as I would like. The knees and legs seem to have some will of their own, but when a pain hits, I have learned to call on Jesus. Mother Rowland told me passages in the bible that addressed everything we will go through on this side of eternity. Mother and I spoke on little things like that and it helped draw us closer to one another. The depths of our talks cannot be summed up in the few pages I have written and some of our conversations are private. God knows we have so many things we can share but some must be kept, for the mystery.

Mother, I love you and thank you for your love, kindness, and above all for revealing to me our Father. God be glorified in all I do, for you are the One I aim to please.

Julia Thomas

Who Can Find a Virtuous Woman?

Mother Emma J. Rowland. She opens her mouth with wisdom; and in her tongue is the law of kindness. Proverbs 31: 10; 26

Her life is crowned with honor and it blooms toward others that love her dearly.

All her doctors enjoy talking with her and are always asking "what is your secret?" Mother's answer is always the same, "Prayer! Prayer! Prayer!" I make sure I keep up with all appointments throughout the year.

She says to me," My latter days are better and I am a grateful woman". Surely God's goodness and mercy follow her daily.

Mother tells me God sent all the right people into her life to fulfill the needs in her livelihood. After she sold her car she did not know how she was going to get about. She said that "God's plan was already provided and Jesus is real and He has been real to me!"

Every day is a gift from God and I've appreciated how Mother has touched my life. When I count my blessings, I am so thankful.

If you want happiness for a lifetime always be willing to help others.

I love you, Mother Rowland,
Joan Hadley

Grace. Amazing Grace!

"Good morning Pastor Boyd, I love you." Oh how I love this sweet, sweet Sunday morning greeting from Rev. Emma Rowland. I have not had the benefit of years of interaction with her, but in the time that we have had, nearly 10 years, I have grown to love this precious angel from God and all that she represents.

A few years ago, I had the privilege of accompanying Rev. Rowland, her daughter, and granddaughter to StoryCorps Atlanta. StoryCorps offers an opportunity for loved ones to record stories that have shaped their lives. Those stories are then archived at the Library of Congress and they may air on National Public Radio. In this particular recording, Rev. Rowland's granddaughter, Cheryl, interviewed her and I was allowed to be a "fly on the wall" in the interview room.

What a blessing it was to share in hearing the story of Rev. Rowland's life! She is a living testimony of God's Grace and Favour! During the StoryCorps' interview, some of the things that stood out to me were Rev. Rowland's practicality, sense of humor, and her toughness. Again, we've not had many opportunities to interact outside of the worship setting so I was unaware of the fact that her grandmother raised her after her mother passed away when she was young. I was unaware of her background as a staunch leader at the Scripto Pen Company in Atlanta. I was unaware of her extensive travel around the world. I was even unaware of how much she was sought after as a speaker at conference events in various places around the country. What a blessing to learn her life story and hear the common thread of "God's Grace" interwoven throughout.

I count it a privilege to offer these words on such a momentous occasion. Ninety-nine years... what a blessing! Ninety-nine years with good health, excellent mental awareness, and great relationships... that is Grace! Amazing Grace! Rev. Rowland is such a precious and sweet woman. What a privilege it is to know her and to love her!

Pastor Christopher L. Boyd, Ph.D. | *Executive Pastor*
Word of Faith Family Worship Cathedral

A Friend Kind of Sister

In the year of 1994, I made my first visit to Word of Faith Family Worship Center (WOF), on a beautiful Sunday morning. The only available parking was way toward the lower end of the parking lot. I was extremely tired, almost to the point of giving out and just when I thought I would not be able to make it to the entrance to the Sanctuary, I looked back and mentally calculated that it was about the same distance to return to my car. I felt I had no choice but to continue walking toward the Church door – however each step was an effort. I looked to my left and a lady was just leaving her car. She looked at me with a cheerful smile and greeted me warmly with "we're so glad to have you this morning" which seemed to give me the strength to go a little further.

I attended her Sunday school class and was strengthened physically as well as Spiritually as she reached out to everyone. We later took a bus trip to a Women of the Word Conference and not by human error but Divine Ordained, we ended up with each of us not having an assigned room-mate. We took the one room that was left together and became prayer partners from that day to this and whenever each of us desire a Word from the Lord, one of us will dial the others phone number and we always experience the presence of Jehovah God.

She is a "Friend Kind of Sister". We both realized that our friendship was clearly ordained of God; over the years, it has grown stronger and stronger. I am so grateful to have such a Woman of Faith in my life; a Woman that walks in Holy and Reverential fear of God. Emma Rowland is a vessel of honor in the eyes of the Almighty Omniscient God.

Strength and Honor are her clothing and
she shall rejoice in the time to come.
She openeth her mouth with Wisdom and
in her tongue is the law of kindness.
Favor is deceitful and beauty is vain;
but a Woman that feareth the Lord, she shall be praised.
Give her the fruit of her hands and
let her own works praise her in the gates.
Proverbs 31:25,26,30,31

I have penned these words under the guidance of the Holy Spirit with much love and with all the sincerity that I am capable.

Donella Cantrell

A Virtuous Woman

I've known Mother Rowland for many years. Did you know she was a seamstress and has always been an active ministry servant in Sunday school and church?

When I think of Mother Rowland, I think of a person who demonstrates and has knowledge of God's Word. She lives His Word. Mother Rowland refuses to show anger or be controlled by it.

Her daily walk with God is evident and desirable. She is precious and has a meek and quiet spirit.

Because of her loving and caring attitude, my children Lita, Juan, and Nina still refer to her as "Grandma Rowland" the name they gave her when they were small children. They loved her and enjoyed going to her house with her grandchildren and my nephews and niece, Joel, Tyrone and Francine Pope.

Her 98th birthday was celebrated in Brooklyn, New York. That's remarkable for a 98 year old woman. Where was she when her granddaughter Francine, who lives there, was trying to locate her? – In Virginia and later in upstate New York. She is still a world traveler!

She is an inspiration to all as she teaches the Word by example and tells of the goodness of God in her life. She is a gift from God.

Mother Rowland, "You have always been an inspiration and a mentor to me."

Wishing you a Happy 99th Birthday!!!

Dorothy G. Cobb

Loving Mother Rowland

Meeting Mother Rowland

It happened at a Sunday morning worship service. Two destinies collided through a melodious symphony of hand clapping, foot tapping, and Hallelujahs resounding from pew to pew. The praise team was singing a song that was reminiscent of hymns my grandfather had led at my home church during devotional service many years earlier. The Spirit of God had made His presence known. Hands were in the air waving in surrender to an invisible God who had somehow captivated the hearts of each congregant.

As I savored the sweetness of the atmosphere, I felt a hand graze the back of my head. Understanding the rapture of the moment, I turned smiling to greet the caught-up worshipper and locked eyes with a short-statured, elderly woman. She quickly apologized for her unintentional contact. Still smiling, I reassured her that no harm had been done. We continued in worship.

At first glance, this endearing lady reminded me of my grandmother. However, looking back I realize that it wasn't her physical attributes that resembled my grandmother, who was much taller and more robust. It was the maternal, caring spirit that I discerned in her that had triggered the connection.

Having had the privilege of growing up in the same home with my grandparents, I developed an affection for seniors. I soon discovered that many of them housed gold mines of untapped wisdom that they would readily share with teachable recipients. I learned to appreciate and respect these seasoned believers for what they offered to our world. Quite naturally I was drawn to this sweet-spirited saint, who I later learned to be Mother Emma Rowland, affectionately known as "Mother Rowland."

The initial touch that I received from Mother Rowland was thought to be a careless nudge resulting from zealous praise. However, today, I know her touch was appointed by God even before the foundation of the world.

"In Him also we have obtained an inheritance, being predestined according to the purpose of Him who works all things according to the counsel of His will."
Ephesians 1:11

"A man's heart plans his way, but the LORD directs his steps."
Proverbs 16:9

Getting to Know Mother Rowland

Once I joined Word of Faith Family Worship Center, I realized I needed to allocate time for God to minister to me. I had served dutifully in my previous church and felt I needed solace and a washing with the water of His Word. While growing up, I had attended Sunday School every Sunday and enjoyed eating from the LORD's table. Valuing this background, I delighted in discovering that Word of Faith, unlike other churches I had visited in the Metro Atlanta area, had a Sunday School Department. Although I tried a couple of classes that were within my age group, I eventually gravitated to my natural inclination to hang out with the older folks.

I walked into the Women of Acts class, and there she was the lively little lady that I met in worship service. I eagerly took a seat not wanting to miss what she had to say. The integrity and sincerity in her heart was undeniable. Week after week, I attended the class, and week after week I was blessed by the simplified message she delivered. Seeing Mother Rowland faithfully render exegesis of the Holy Scripture was especially moving and inspirational.

On occasion, Mother Rowland would share her testimony of being denied the privilege of serving as a minister of the Gospel of Jesus Christ simply because she was a woman. Her story, when carefully examined, reveals a woman of strength, character and a steadfast love for God. I say this because many of us know someone who has left church for a lesser offense than blatant rejection. No one could really blame her if she chose to jump ship. Yet, she maintained her resolve to stir-up the gift of God that resided inside her, regardless of the naysayers. Man's rejection undoubtedly hurt her, but it did not impede her from blooming where she was planted. It delayed her ultimate call to ministry, but it could not deny it. Her love for God compelled her to continue serving God in whatever capacity deemed permissible for her gender, which inevitably led her to teach Sunday School. Of course, God had a plan. He always gets the glory in the end. Today, Rev. Emma Rowland is an ordained minister of the Gospel of Jesus Christ. What an awesome story of trust and triumph!

> *"Therefore, my beloved brethren, be steadfast, unmovable, always abounding in the work of the Lord, knowing that your labor is not in vain in the Lord."*
> 1 Corinthians 15:58

Admiring Mother Rowland

Mother Rowland's sweetness and subservient demeanor belie the fact that she has experienced a myriad of challenges and disappointments throughout her life. Nonetheless, she does not wear her problems on her sleeves, instead she gets on her knees and carries them to our Abba Father – Daddy, God. Her prayer life is certainly evident by the life she has lived.

I have witnessed Mother Rowland's faithfulness to God while enduring sickness. I remember visiting her in the hospital to pray and encourage her. I prayed for God's healing and strength to manifest in her body. She in turn beseeched heaven on my behalf while lying in a hospital bed. Who does that? Such a selfless act could only originate from a person who has died to self and is alive to the purposes of Christ in her life.

Mother Rowland has pressed her way through the deaths of her husband, sons, relatives, and close friends, along with enduring church hurt and personal sickness. Yet, she miraculously maintains a more-than-a-conqueror mindset, choosing to trust God's character even when she cannot at times comprehend His plan. Even more, she chooses not to complain or compare herself to others. She is driven by her love for Christ who provokes her to love others. She does all of this while maintaining a light-hearted, humorous attitude.

Rev. Rowland's responses to adversity have been lessons in and of themselves. She proclaims without opening her mouth that **I trust God**. It is as if you can hear her saying, "I am hurt, but I am still trusting God. I don't understand, but I am still trusting God. I can't see my way out, but I am still trusting God." Instinctively, God being God will never allow any of His children to be *put to shame* for hoping in Him. For the Scripture declares,

> *"Whoever believes on Him will not be put to shame."*
> Romans 9:33; 10:11

> *"Do not fear, for you will not be ashamed; neither be disgraced, for you will not be put to shame."*
> Isaiah 54:4

Loving Mother Rowland

Time has a way of unveiling hidden things. This is true with a person's potential, shortcomings and character. To date, I have known Mother Rowland astonishingly for seventeen years; yet, time has not diminished the gracefulness and impact of this quiet-spirited giant in God's Kingdom. In truth, it has amplified the potency of her sweetness and steadfastness in the Lord.

To hear that a person is "steadfast in the Lord" can sound like an empty compliment until a crisis arises in your own circumstances that puts you on the search for someone of a similar caliber. With the passing of time, Mother Rowland's character has proven credible and consistent. Her display of confidentiality and approachability makes her a sought after counselor for a host of troubled people.

I recall the time when I was literally crushed in my spirit as a result of an unsubstantiated reproach made against me. I was instinctively drawn to Mother Rowland, who I had only known a short while, having imbibed her benevolent spirit. Because I chose not to disclose names and the specifics of the situation, she did not attempt to dig for the juicy details. Though she did not know the particulars, she did perceive the hurt in my eyes. Her maternal instincts immediately kicked in. She prayed, comforted and encouraged me which ultimately revived my trodden spirit. I thank God for her graciousness and tact in the matter. Since that time, I have come to appreciate her as an advocate, counsellor, mentor and constant encourager.

Mother Rowland expresses her love in such a tangible way that it is hard to ignore. It's the kind of love that is bestowed unashamedly. It yells... I LOVE YOU, AND I DON'T CARE WHO KNOWS IT! It's the sort of love our soul craves. It is the love our Heavenly Father has for us and instructs us to have for each other. Having experienced this love, it is only natural to reciprocate it.

To know her is to love her. Weight has been added to this legendary cliché as it relates to Mother Rowland. Anyone who has invested the time to walk alongside her can truly attest to its accuracy. Knowing who Mother Rowland is in Christ has instinctively led me and others to love and adore her.

Without question, believers have been commissioned to love one another. Yet, because of the idiosyncrasies, habits, and odd behaviors of some people, we sometimes find ourselves struggling to obey this command and having to rely heavily upon the Holy Spirit to empower us to do so. Loving Mother Rowland, on the contrary, is stress-free and joyous. It is calming to the soul. Giving is reciprocal and meaningful in the relationship. This does not mean that it is a gift for a gift. As a matter of fact, Mother Rowland's gifts most often are not material things. Her gifts come in the form of prayers, encouragements, and a judge-free, listening ear. It is simply love responding to love. Mother Rowland is a true blessing from God, and I am so grateful to have been chosen to share a portion of her life.

> *"Every good and every perfect gift is from above, and comes down from the Father of lights, with whom there is no variation or shadow of turning."*
> James 1:17

I love you!
Sharon Bradley

She makes her Children Feel Special and Loved

I have known Mother Rowland, (Mother), since 1993 when I moved to Atlanta from Bessemer, Alabama to work for the Southern Tennis Association. In fact, I met her when I began to worship at Word of Faith Church. Mother Rowland was my Sunday School teacher and Bible Study teacher on Tuesday Night for the Women's Class. At this time, the church was located at Ben Hill Road. We developed a connection through the Holy Spirit at once and communicated by telephone frequently. Mother Rowland expounded on the biblical word in a gentle and thorough manner. She knew the Bible both Old and New Testament in a very detailed manner. Many of the students in both classes would ask Mother questions and she would quote the Bible and made it applicable and real in every situation. Mother Rowland was a Mother to all the students in both classes and conducted herself in a superb but humble manner. Mother made all the students feel special and loved as though she was our real and actual mother. Mother developed the name of Mother because she treated all her students wonderfully special and uniquely individually as her own child. Apparently, I am still excited about my magnificent experience with Mother in both of the above mentioned classes.

Mother and I became prayer partners and the beautiful Godly relationship grew in an awesome way. Consequently, my actual Mother passed away and Mother Rowland was there when I needed someone to talk to and to cry with at this hugely difficult point of my life. I remember staying at Mother's house many days and she would make me a wonderful kool-aid that was so tasty and loving. Every time I visited her, I was expecting to drink a glass of her kool-aid and some sweet potato pie. Mother is still by Atlanta.

I have been living in California since 2001, and Mother and I still communicate by telephone regularly. In fact, I am still seeking Godly advice from her and cherish the moments that I can receive good sound Godly principles to assist me with my daily walk with God. Yes!!!

In 2008, I left a gigantic government job to follow my passion in order to teach TENNIS. Lordy!! That was a big move for me to step out on faith and leave behind a huge paying job for literally peanuts in the beginning. However, I kept calling Mother and praying. Currently, I am still teaching tennis and calling Mother and praying!!!!

Mother is a God fearing and loving woman of God. I am so glad that the Lord God Almighty brought me through Atlanta and I met Mother. She exudes the faith of one of the prophets of the Bible. She has always been an excellent listener and powerful thinker that would provide you with her best for your life. I am delighted to provide the above words regarding my experience with her and I am looking forward to many years of the above with Mother.

Mother Rowland is the best I have met in terms of a sound and close relationship with God and I am extremely privileged to note the above.

Thank you very much!!!!
Linda Paulding

Our Heavenly Father has blessed us with a wonderful woman of God with her unique qualities and devotion in the ministry. My fond memories are the many times we prayed together saying, "Prayer is the key and faith unlocks the door".

Minister Mary Bell

Reverend Emma Jane Rowland

THE PATH TO HER PRESENCE

For some time now, I have been acutely aware of the fact that I am on a high stakes search for my destiny. I have read the Bible in many different ways and through the eyes of many different authors and I have done it many times. What I have discovered is that God has a plan and He unveils it His way, in His time, and through His choices.

I can recall many things that could have played a part in getting me from where I was to where I am but one introduction stands out and it was the unlikely introduction to my friend, confidant, and spiritual jewel, **Reverend Emma Jane Rowland.**

I met her at Word of Faith Family Worship Cathedral (WOF). I did not just show up at WOF, I was led there over a time span of 12 years. (I had no knowledge that Mother Rowland even existed until the appointed time in 2003. It was by no means a direct encounter.

The initial encounter was with **the late Nathaniel H. Bronner, Sr.**, in 1991, via a declining marriage destined to fail. It was probably the most pivotal occurrence in the marriage for me. For the life of me, I can't remember why we met with Mr. Bronner at his office in West End in Atlanta, Georgia. What I do remember is the wisdom, the kindness, the smile, the utter angelic demeanor of this great man. The meeting lasted about two hours and **the three of us** talked about everything including and especially golf. I don't play golf, nor do I understand it but he talked about it with such fervor, that at that time, I seriously considered it to the point of signing up for lessons. Not to be!

Though he did not pass away until 1993, I never saw Mr. Bronner again. The source of the introduction is no longer a part of my life (divorced in September 1991) yet the experience lingered.

INTRODUCTION TO DALE C. BRONNER
(The son of the kind man)

One night as I prepared for bed with the television set on **AIB** as usual, around 11:30 p.m. up popped the name and likeness of Dale C. Bronner.

My immediate thought was his last name; he was an extension of this great and kind man **Nathaniel H. Bronner, Sr.** So I watched and internalized the message and every message since then in which I have access. His messages are timely and always appear to speak into my life. I thought, *"He is a chip off of the old block."* I discovered he had a church in East Point. I told everyone I knew, about my new discovery.

I respected and admired both of the Bronners (father and son). I did visit the church to experience the son in person, but the distance was a deterrent for me. I chose to experience the messages on AIB as I was unwilling to drive to 2435 Ben Hill Rd in East Point where WOF was originally located. I was determined to find a church that was no more than three miles away from my home.

GOD BROUGHT THE CHURCH TO ME

In 2002 I experienced a very traumatic and devastating loss that in my mind, re-arranged my soul. It was at this time I was desperately seeking a Word from God. I knew the Bible and wanted to know it more. I was visiting different churches in search for a leadership replica of WOF.

I actually did a class project during a Corporate Coaching class under the leadership of Nancy Allen, MA, RCC Coach/Facilitator at Impact Training & Development, Inc. I chose a project to define the perfect church, at that time, it was the only thing on my mind. When I finished the project, it was WOF but it was missing a very important element, it was too far, (approximately 18 miles).

Then one Saturday morning as I sat on my deck reading the newspaper, I saw a headline **"WOF to Move to Cobb County!"** I could not believe it; I called everyone I knew to tell them that God brought the church to me. It was to have its temporary origin at a former Sam's Club building at 150 Riverside Parkway. I actually got in my car and measured it. It was exactly three miles from my home!

The first available Sunday I was there! When the doors of the church opened, I walked through!! I called Nancy, the Corporate Coach facilitator and informed her that my project had been completed! God had brought the church to me!

THE INTRODUCTION TO MOTHER ROWLAND

Being a certified teacher, facilitator, and sales person, I envisioned my first assignment would be to teach a Sunday school class. There was a gentleman there by the name of Mr. Brown. After looking at my documentation, he looked at me and said, I have just the right assignment for you. He assigned me to the Sunday School Class of Mother Rowland. Of course, I was disappointed as I felt I was destined to teach. In addition, it was an all women's class and I prefer a co-ed class. However, God had other plans. I went to the class as directed and I have no regrets. She was as angelic as Nathaniel H. Bronner, Sr.

HER WISDOM WAS PERVASIVE

I took a seat right in front of her as she taught. If she dropped a tissue, I was there to pick it up. There was more wisdom in her movements than most people's words. Each Sunday after church, I looked forward to experiencing her in Sunday School.

I SHOWED UP ONE DAY & SHE WAS NOT THERE!

Since at the time, I had no personal relationship with her, I had no way of knowing what was going on. Then **Sharon Bradley** came in and announced to the class that Mother Rowland was in the hospital. She had attended an event by T.D. Jakes, and had to be rushed to Piedmont Hospital. She said, she would have more information next week. Not for me, I knew where Piedmont was and I knew I was not going to wait a week. When class was over, I went straight to Piedmont.

"I AM NOT SCARED, I KNOW MY GOD"~ Rev Rowland

As I walked down the long hallway, I tried to imagine what I would say to her as I did not have that type of personal relationship with her. When I got to her room, I walked in. She turned over, looked at me, and said "I knew it was you; I heard your footsteps."

I sat down and told her how I knew she was there and she told me what happened. After being there a while; in walked **Rev John Williams, of WOF**. As he spoke with her regarding her condition and her concerns, she immediately said: *"I am not scared, I know my God!"*

We all prayed together. That was the beginning of what has become a very intimate relationship. It lasted a good part of 30 days in all. Daily, I went to visit with her and to give her daughter Vera, who was very protective, a break. At one point, I was so protective that Vera reminded me that it was 'her' mother lying there. LOL! Mother Rowland laughed at us as we volleyed for possession of her attention.

ONE DAY I WENT THERE AND VERA WAS DISTRAUGHT

The doctor had informed her that Mother Rowland had taken a turn for the worse. He asked her to call family members. They were moving her to intensive care. The doctor was attempting to get her to sign a document; I think it was called a DNR. Vera refused to sign it. She said she was not giving up. The doctor was very persuasive but he was no match for Vera.

GOD CALLING ME TO PRAY

The next day, God woke me up with an urgent command to go and pray for her. I was to dress with precision and to get there ASAP. When I got to the hospital, I had missed Vera by seconds. Mother Rowland was asleep, unconscious, or otherwise unaware that I was there. I did not want to startle her.

I sat next to her and began to sing. As I stood over her singing, praying and crying, her eyes opened up and she said "you are a very beautiful woman." The next statement she made was change the TV Channel to the gospel channel; (she told me the channel).

The next day, when I came to the hospital, I saw the doctor that attempted to get Vera to sign the DNR. He was sitting outside of the room and we looked at each other. He said: "I don't know what happened." I said: Prayer happened. There are a multitude of people praying for this woman and Prayer Works. He simply dropped his head and continued his report. Eventually, she was released.

I WANT TO OPEN SOME DRAWERS!

She continued to improve as she moved in with Vera. One day I went over there and she said she was ready to go home. She said she was very respectful of other people's privacy and she did not ramble. She said she wanted to go home and open some drawers....it is exactly what happened. She went home and to this day, she lives independently, teaches, and preaches.

THE REST IS HISTORY

It has been over 10 years. In that time, Mother Rowland has become my friend and confidant. We spend hours talking about everything. Always, she uses the vocabulary of the Bible. I told her that if she had a nosy neighbor, they would think we were gossiping as we talked and dialogued about Moses, David, and other exciting Biblical characters and events.

SHE IS A POSTER CHILD FOR CHRISTIAN LIVING

In all of these years, she never ever speaks without infusing God into her comments. As wise as she is, she always inquires as if she could learn something. If you give her a compliment, she immediately acknowledges that it is God's Grace. She has the wisdom of a woman and the Spirit of a teenager. Because of her, I am a better person.

God says in Jeremiah 29:11, *"I know the plans I have for you"*. He goes on in Isaiah 55:8 to say *"My thoughts and ways are not your thoughts and ways"*. Bishop Bronner and most respectable leaders speak of the appointed time. In the end, God says, the secret things belong to Him. *"The hidden things belong to the LORD our God, but the revealed things belong to us and our children forever, so that we may follow all the words of this law."* Deuteronomy 29:29~HCSB

While I don't know what is waiting down the road, God has demonstrated time and time again, that what He has for us must be discovered. I am alert, expectant, and grateful. On the way to my destiny, God has chosen to share what has to be one of his favorites in the name of **Reverend Emma Jane Rowland**...I shall stay tuned for God's "After this.."

Ivory Dorsey, Sunday, July 26, 2015

Faithful

Mother Rowland has been such a positive and inspiring part of my life. Her words of encouragement have meant so much to me. After teaching combined Sunday School one day, she told me, "You are exactly who and what I thought you were. Continue to let the Lord use you." Those words will forever stay with me. Mother Rowland is such a caring person. Our relationship has grown to the point that she calls me her son. I do not take it lightly that she considers me a part of her family.

When I think of her, the word faithful comes to mind. Even at her age, she is always at church on Sunday morning with a smile on her face and love in her heart for all. She is the example that we should all strive to emulate. Mother Rowland is a true treasure. I thank God for her life and the impact she's had on mine.

I love you Mother!

May God continue to smile upon you and his blessings continue to overtake you.

She's the solid foundation of life,
which automatically falls into place

Lifting herself above and beyond normal expectations,
wisdom glows from her face

The mother of reasoning and a strong partner
to man's decisions, she's a vital part of the
completion of our religion

Intuition's a main part of her shield, surrendering
her heart for her faith in God is real

The load may be heavy and the road may
lead her in many directions

But never will she compromise the duty of true affection

Holding together family and others in needs

Pureness in her heart to give rather than receive

Sacrifice, never giving it a second thought,
it comes naturally

She sleeps in the bed of Jesus, not fictional but factual

She's without a price

Embracing everything good in her life

Walking in steps which God has laid

A true spiritual being,
she is the center with love never to fade

Believing in the Lord, she lives in a world without doubt

Understanding God and what life is truly about

Faithful, honest, she has built a home in the truth

A gift from God to pass on to you

She will comfort, always there to open her
heart with an undeniable love

A virtuous woman, given to the world
from the father above

For she's the caretaker, and the main ingredient of life

The (VIRTUOUS WOMAN) a strong
symbol standing for all that is right.
L.P. ,2004

Love,
Rodney D. Moss
Assistant Superintendent of the Word of
Faith Sunday School.

Then Just Watch Me

She turned toward me, stood flat footed, looked me eyeball to eyeball and out it came.

I'll never forget the challenge presented to me by a then almost 80 year old, seemingly frail, little woman with a sweet unassuming smile. Only this time she wasn't smiling. She meant every one of the four words she said.

We served together in the Sunday school ministry for nearly three years. My title was superintendent but I was actually her student!

She appealed to me because she allowed me to be myself. I am unpretentious and I love to laugh. Usually women Mother Emma Rowland's age don't have or make time for laughter because life is too serious, time is running out and they've been through too much, and yet my connection with the woman of God was first made through joy and laughter.

Don't get me wrong, Mother has a serious side, but she'll still double over with laughter if something is genuinely funny.

She had returned to Sunday school after a serious illness. I believe she had taken ill while attending a TD Jakes conference and rushed to the hospital from there. It seemed to take forever for her to recover and get well. Let's face it, she was at an age where if she HAD gone to be with the Lord, it could have justly been said, "she lived a long and fruitful life." But apparently God wasn't through with her yet. HALLELUJAH!

When she finally did return to church, we hugged and I cried. She kept saying to me, "Baby, God is holy", over and over and over, "Baby, God is holy." Before I could begin to feel self-conscious but NOT before conviction set in, she went into a praise and worship that set me on fire.

We had church right there in the church hallway. And then when THAT was all said and done, we went into a holy laughter and could barely stop. When we finally came to ourselves, we turned to go wherever we were headed, each in her own direction.

I started thinking...what I wouldn't give to be like that at her age. She was full of life and vibrant, balanced and well ...just awesome.

I turned back around and said, "Mother Rowland, when I grow up, I want to be like you." She turned toward me, stood flat footed, looked me eyeball to eyeball and said in that very strong voice, "then just watch me."

The apostle Paul said in Philippians 4:9

> *"Those things, which he have both learned and received,*
> *and heard, and seen in me, do:*
> *and the God of peace shall be with you."*

When I grow up, I want to live a life where I too can offer that challenge to younger women.

Praise God for Mother Emma Rowland

Dr. Linda Chinn

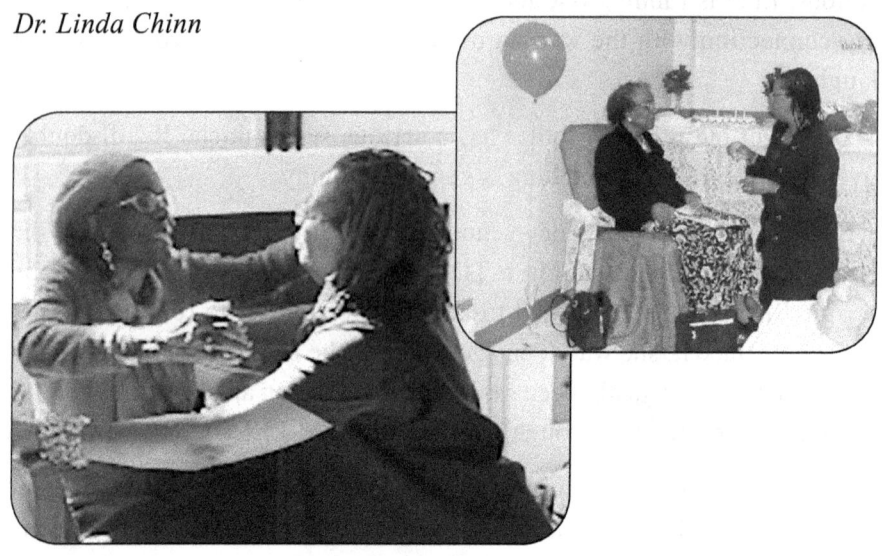

God Still Had Work for Her to Do

It has truly been an honor knowing and learning from you these seventeen years.

I first met Mother in 1998 when our church was still in the old location on Ben Hill Rd. It was shortly after my own mother had passed from a long illness and Mother made an announcement one Sunday about Women's Daily Walk that met on Tuesday nights at the church. I felt in my heart God wanted me to be there because it was Tuesdays that I would be with my mom and now this would fill those days.

From the time Mother Rowland and I met, we were inseparable. I would meet her and a couple of other ladies at the church on Saturday mornings to clean the church and when I was at work if I was having a hard day I would call her and get her to pray with me. On my off days I would pick her up and we would spend the whole day together, sometimes shopping and other times talking, reading the bible or praying about things I was going through. She would always let me vent then she would tell me what the Word said and then we would pray. I always felt at ease and able to talk to Mother about anything that was on my mind.

I have always felt that God sent Mother into mine and my daughter's lives. She has been a true blessing to me and I hope I have been the same for her. I would joke with her son Homer and her daughter Vera that I was taking their mother for my own but they would just say they were used to sharing her with others.

I remember when she and Homer were in the hospital at the same time and Homer went on to be with the Lord and mother recovered, my heart ached for her and her family, but God still had work for her to do. Since then she has adopted many more daughters and sons in Christ and I miss all my quality time with her but as Vera and Homer said we must share.

Love You Forever
Joyce Simpson

Your Spiritual Son & Daughter's Birthday Tribute

I remember being in the choir loft at Word of Faith Family Worship Center in East Point, GA more than 23 years ago and peering down among the congregants to see a little woman seated near the front of the church, at the end of the pew, always immersed in the message, the music, and the Bible she held in her lap.

You couldn't help but notice the intensity of her worship as she listened to the choir sing and to the message being preached. There was something about her that made you want to know her – and to know more about her.

My husband also served as an Usher during those early years, and almost every Sunday, he would be stationed in the aisle just next to where Mother would be seated, so as time passed, they actually formed a loving bond with one another long before I had gotten a chance to meet her. It was sometime later, after we'd all become closer, that she told him that she would see an angel standing beside him each week when he served in that spot.

After a few weeks of observing her from afar, I finally met her for myself. I soon discovered that she was soft spoken yet eloquent in speech, and firm in her conviction for Christ. She was unassuming in her demeanor, but she was a bold and powerful witness for God. It was evident that she was humble and didn't have a need to be 'front-n-center', nor always to be seen or recognized by others, but rather she carried herself in such a graceful manner that you couldn't help but single her out and admire her Godly qualities. And although we were never quite sure of her age back then (at the time she wouldn't reveal her age because as she shared with us later, she didn't want to be treated like an 'old lady'!), for years it remained a guessing game between my husband and me.

As the months progressed, I got to know her so much better through intimate visits at her home and ours, and through some interesting phone conversations. I grew immensely attached to her warm spirit, and motherly presence [which has always been especially meaningful to me since at the time, my own Mother resided in another state]. Mother Rowland and I talked together, prayed together, and even cried together for hours – no topic was off limits! How refreshing, I thought, to share my thoughts and concerns with a truly seasoned saint without judgment of any kind; just to receive her kind and loving instruction by the Word of God. Throughout the years, the two of us have claimed victory over many situations that have arisen between us and for others.

One of the greatest teachable moments for my life has been to sit in her Sunday School class. Teaching with such clarity and authority in the Holy Ghost, she has always made the Word of God come alive. For a short while I served as one of her many protégés in that she would allow me to facilitate the class in her stead on designated Sundays. Serving in that capacity greatly impacted my life as it gave me more time to spend with her whenever we would study each week's lesson together. I was humbled to serve in that capacity for the years that I did as I was assured that she was always interceding for me, and quietly giving me a mother's approval through God's Grace.

In addition to our relationship through Sunday School, she has also supported and participated in other fellowships such as the Upper Room meetings that used to be held in our home. Founded by Roslyn Foreman and Selena Peoples, she served as a spiritual counselor and facilitator at many of those meetings in which groups of all ages met to discuss the Word of God, pray, and fellowship afterwards. And ever the consummate teacher, she always came prepared to expound upon the Word with meekness but with God-given authority. I think it became evident to me even then that Mother Rowland was never one to be content at sitting at home, but that she enjoyed being around others – especially others of like-minded faith regardless of their ages.

Many years ago, Bishop Bronner preached a message wherein he stated that everyone needs a 'Paul' (a spiritual advisor & teacher); a 'Barnabus' (a truthful friend & trusted confidant); and a 'Timothy' (a protégé) in their life. My husband and I remain blessed to consider Mother Rowland as both a 'Paul' and 'Barnabus' in our lives for she has been a great mentor and trusted friend to both of us. There's no one whom we trust as much to be faithful to call our names out in prayer, and with whom we can share our inner-most feelings – all the while being assured that those feelings are always held in confidence.

Over the years, we've been blessed to experience anytime prayers and late night phone conversations and consultations with her; we've received beautiful and memorable hand-written personal notes of her expressions of love toward us, not to mention the purposeful visits she's made to our homes – each time to declare God's blessings, peace, and prosperity over us and our abode. We've also shared many loving meals together; including a lot of Church®'s fried chicken! And lastly, she continues to shower us with her boundless love which has meant volumes to us as individuals and as a married couple!

Not much has changed over the ensuing years. Mother, you are still a humble, loving, and giving Servant of God. You remain our teacher, mentor, spiritual Mother and friend, and a great influence in both our lives and Christian walk. And so it is with joy that we look forward to celebrating your birthday with you once again while continuing to witness for ourselves the hand and Grace of God upon your life. We will always continue to thank God for your spirit; your love; your walk of faith; and your example of Christian service to God (first and always), and to your extended family and friends. We also thank your daughter, Vera, and your granddaughter, Cheryl, for numbering us among family to share in your life and love, and allowing us to call you 'Mother', too!

Happy Birthday, Mother!

We love and honor you each day…and always!

Your Other Son & Daughter,
Deacon Stephen L. and
Karen R. Bradfield

Your Praying Spirit Gives Me Hope

Mother Emma Rowland, since April 2000, you have been my only Sunday School Women of Acts teacher other than Sharon, Dee Dee and Melvina. This is the only class that I have ever attended in my 15 years as a Word of Faith Family member because of your unique teaching style. Your passion for the Word of God shows every time you are teaching a lesson in class or interceding for someone in need. Mother, I love how you interpret the scripture with an explanation of the lesson and then encourage other members and visitors to participate with their interpretation of the lessons which lead you to give a response or implementing an action.

For example, in 2012, you spoke about families and fellowship and how we should treat one another with love and respect in and out of church. Then one of our members, Mary Purnell, decided to speak on your comment, she said, "I have been attending the Women of Acts class for some time and the only people I know are Mother Rowland and Ramona by name. It would be great if I could know other people in the class by name when I see them in and out of church. You immediately responded that we used to have name tags for each person in class and we need to start it again. Once you made that request, the Women of Acts class has been providing name tags for members and visitors ever since.

Mother Rowland, I consider you as my second mother because you see me as your daughter. I truly love you because of your praying spirit that gives me hope; positive words that encourage me to excel; listening ear that causes me to focus; sense of humor that makes my heart rejoice; loving smile that brings me peace; tender thoughts that lift my spirit; supporting heart that believes I can do all thing through Christ who strengthens me and a gracious attitude that makes me feel appreciated.

I believed that our Lord Jesus Christ placed you in my life to give me hope that my later years are only going to get better. No weapon formed against me will profit and I hold true to your saying from God's Word that He that is in me is greater than he that is in the world!

Ramona Battle

The Godmother AKA Babycakes

Godmother, is a title usually given to a woman designated by one's parents to care for a child in the event that the parents are unable to do so. A Godmother is also a prominent person who plays an integral part of the spiritual and social milestones of the child.

My birth parents were long departed from the earthly realm when Emma Rowland came into my life. I used to tell people that I adopted her, but more and more I have come to believe that my Heavenly Father chose Mommy to care for me, guide me, love me and to be an integral part of not just my Spiritual and Social milestones, but my life in general.

How did it begin? That is a difficult question to answer. Oh, I know when, where, and the circumstances through which I first met Emma Rowland. If I calculate the year that I began attending "Word of Faith Christian Church", I would say the relationship began in 1999.

I began attending Word of Faith Family Worship Center sometime in 1999. I had been raised in a church where I attended Sunday school as a child, had attended in my previous church and I was glad to know that the tradition was continued there. I wandered the halls and eventually found the class of women. I took my seat and gave the small elderly lady standing in front of the class my full attention. I was amazed at the agility of her mind and body as she elaborated on the theme of the week. She quoted scriptures to make her point that were not even in the book. She asked us questions and related the discussion to present day situations. I marveled at her boldness and frank comparisons of the everyday issues of greed, lust and deceit whenever the biblical character was struggling with such a sin.

This little dynamo did not bite her tongue when it came to unveiling hidden sin. While she was kind and listened compassionately to any of the sisters who had personal struggles, she also let us know that hidden sin would destroy us and affect our relationship with God, but she was never judgmental. I knew right away, that I wanted this Godly woman in my life. I knew that I could give her permission to see the real me. I wanted her to know the struggles and desires of my heart even when they failed to earn sainthood. I felt that she could help me to become a better mother and a stronger, more dedicated woman of God.

Well, it wasn't long before Mother Rowland's class was too large and they divided the class into an older women's group and a younger women's group. I was told that I wasn't old enough to stay. I obediently moved to the younger group. I don't think I was in that class a month. I made my way back to Mother Rowland. I decided I would just "slip" in the back and listen to her sage wisdom. I didn't comment or answer any of the discussion questions because I didn't want to be asked to leave and go to my assigned class.

The next Sunday I slipped in again but a do-gooder informed me that I was too young for the class and I would have to leave. After every class there were women gathered around Mother Rowland, some asking for prayer, other asking questions about the lesson and still others hanging back until they could be alone with the little old lady.

I waited in the corner of the room farthest away from Mother Rowland and the woman she was speaking with. I could see that theirs was a private discussion. When it was my turn to speak with the small statured woman that I admired so much, I was nervous. After all, I was going to ask this pillar of the church to break a rule. Would she go against the policy set forth by the almighty hand of Dale Bronner, the founding Pastor of the church? Would she allow me to stay in her class or would she give a stern lecture about obedience to the under Shepard of the "house". I didn't know, but I had to take the chance and ask.

"Mrs. Rowland, I don't want to go to the class for younger women. I want to stay in your class. I won't learn anything in that other class and I don't have anything in common with those people." I wonder what I was thinking I had in common with ladies that were much older than I? Their leader, Emma Rowland was more than 30 years my senior. I will never forget what she said, "Well you don't have to leave, you can stay right here in this class, you will be 'the baby'."

I have been her baby-girl ever since then.

When I didn't know how to deal with my oldest daughter's marital issues, I went to her and she eloquently told me to "bud out". Along with the "bud out" Mother explained how my relationship with my daughter would be hampered forever if I interfered. Before she explained that my daughter would side with her husband once they made up, she explained that God was the originator of marriage and that He intended that my daughter and her husband find their own way – right or wrong, good or bad. I understood why she told me to "bud out" and I never interfered with the couple. Years later, when that marriage dissolved, I was glad that I took mother's advice. The issues in that marriage have no bearing on the relationship between my son-in-law and me. I remain a good and trusted friend in that young man's life.

When I was presented with a 3 carat engagement ring, mother was the first person I showed it to. It was just something about the way she looked at my finger and then, at me. Even though the only thing she said was, "Chile, he must really love you" those few words gave me pause. I listened to what she said and remembered that look on her face. I thought to myself, "With the exception of giving me this ring, what else has he done that is indicative of "love"? As I thought about it, I began looking for evidence of the young man's declaration of love. Alas, he did not have anything else in his love account for me. I studied him and realized that he did not love me at all. More importantly, he did not love God. I broke the engagement.

As time progressed, mother became my favorite companion. I was a single mother running a busy solo medical practice. I didn't have a lot of time to spend socially with friends. When I could go out, it was with Mother Rowland. If there was a movie premiering, I would call her up and ask her if she wanted to go.

We went to every one of Tyler Perry's plays and movies. We cried and laughed. We gasped in unison when injustices were heaved on the innocent victims and punched clinched fists at the villains. We whispered to the heroines when they missed God's best for them and cheered when they got it right. We sang and got teary eyed when an old spiritual was sung by one of the actors.

Sometimes I just asked her to dinner. I just wanted to be near her. Sometimes I would ask her advice about something and other times she would unlock a biblical truth. Our conversation was so easy, we always seemed to incorporate something about our mutual, One True Love, Jesus Christ.

I never planned to discuss Him with her. He was just such an intricate part of both our lives. He just kept turning up. After I would drop Mother Rowland off at her home, I always marveled about how much divine revelation could be discovered; just talking!

We started a yearly pilgrimage to Chicago, just before spring. We would leave Atlanta just before it got warm and traveled to winter to attend the Christian Working Women's Conference. No matter where I relocated to, Texas or New York, we would meet up for our yearly conference. Sometimes my cousin, Theresa, would join us and sometimes it was just Mommy and me. When her knees began to give her trouble, Mommy, whom I call Babycakes, needed to use a wheelchair. We didn't miss a beat. I will never forget the years I had back surgery and we both had to be in wheel chairs! My cousin had a hard time keeping up on foot! We had a ball!

We would typically arrive on a Thursday. (A day ahead of our fellow pilgrims). I thought that would give me a chance to rest up from my demanding medical practice and be ready for the conference which started with prayer at 7:30 every morning. Whatever was I thinking? There would be no rest for the weary. Babycakes may have arthritic knees but that did not stop her. I would rent a car and after checking in, it was off to Walmart to "stock the room". Chips of various kinds, fruit, cookies and of course chocolate and soda pop. We would also purchase a George Foreman grill. If we didn't like the breakfast or if we missed dinner or lunch and didn't have time to go out between sessions, we just bought whatever meat we wanted and cooked right in the Westin, The Hyatt or the Hilton-wherever we were. I would secretly be laughing my head off when Vera, her daughter, would give me her instructions about what to feed Mother after her bowel problem. For those 4 days, she ate what she wanted and when she wanted and we dared the Devil to interfere.

I am eternally grateful to Vera for praying Babycakes through the bowel ordeal. I was in Texas and for some reason, unreachable by phone. Maybe it was best I didn't know how sick she was. They probably would have banned me from the hospital because of my demands of the hospital staff and physicians.

No matter what conference we went to, the little ole lady was always the first to rise. The first few years of conferences I used to think, "I will skip one of the meetings and just sleep" - not with that 98 pound Dynamo, I didn't. She would be up at least 2 hours before the sessions talking about "We don't want to be late". I started joking with my cousin Theresa when she still worked, that Mother used to store up energy for the whole year, while we would be working, and that's why we would want to rest and she didn't.

And let us not forget the mall runs. One year I threatened not to rent a car, because I was the one who worked the longest hours arriving to the conference needing to sleep and Mother and Theresa would invariably need something from the mall and I would have to Chauffer them. I always rented the car. I never fell asleep, and I never failed to have the time of my life watching Mother shop. Well into her nineties she wanted a pair of red heeled pumps....and she got them!

I cannot express my great joy watching her almost hanging out of the car taking pictures as I rounded the steep mountainside in Colorado. She was just like a kid. Initially she wanted me to take the pictures-while I was driving. She was so excited, I think she forgot that I couldn't take the pictures and perform the curvy mountainside climb.

True to her usual self, she didn't even get jet lag when we went to Colorado! There I was, literally passed out across the bed in the hotel and I felt something pulling my toe. It was Babycakes."Come on, it is time to go. We're going to be late". Unbeknownst to her, my cousin and I talked about alternating who would go to the sessions with her. Among ourselves we came up with a plan that one of us would sleep while the other one went to the session. We never did it though. I didn't want to miss spending time with her.

New York and her 98th Birthday was a highlight! At Brooklyn Tabernacle 10,000 people celebrated her birthday singing Happy Birthday to You.

One of my long term Brooklynite friends, Leslie, gave her the grand tour of New York City. He drove to 4 of the burrows including the Bronx,

Brooklyn, Queens, Manhattan and China Town. We ended that trip with a train ride to Rochester from New York.

Once in Rochester, she set about helping make my newly acquired house a home. Just like any mother, she scrubbed cabinets and light fixtures to get my new home ready for habitation. I expected her to sit in the recliner and watch. Why I expected her not to participate is a mystery. I came into the kitchen and there she was, scrubbing down a kitchen cabinet. Even though I have lived on my own since I was 16 years old, I had never had a mother help me clean a house that was soon to be my home. Isn't that what moms do?

Over the past years, we have traveled other places and had many conversations. Just at as I initially suspected, I can tell Emma Rowland absolutely ANYTHING! When I strayed off of the straight and narrow, she did not miss a beat. She still gave me unconditional love without condemnation. She never said my behavior was right. She always gently reminded me that God expected me to be Holy and Godly. Sometimes, she just launched into telling me a story about a temptation in her life and how she overcame it. As our relationship flourished and her Godly wisdom began to merge with my Spirit, I didn't have tales of mistakes I'd make needing her to support me on the journey back to feeling "right with God". I started talking things over with Mommy BEFORE I was in the temptation. As with any rewarding relationship, there was give and take. There were times when I had to pray for Mother. At least once, God gave me a word for her and I had to ask her a few tough questions or challenge her to look deeper than the surface of a situation.

I became so comfortable with her being "in my business", there were times I told her about things that were headed to a temptation that I didn't even know existed. For example, I might call, just to chit chat and catch up. As I would chat away, telling her whatever was happening at the time, she would see a potential trap of the evil one and advise me not to continue on that path. I would assure her that action was now aborted. I would agree with her wholeheartedly, then able to see the looming danger. I would give the impression that she was confirming what I already knew- STOP! DANGER! THE BRIDGE IS OUT!

After hanging up the telephone, however, I would be almost speechless. How did she see the danger in something I thought was harmless? I hadn't even known I was on the footpath to the bridge, never mind being about to step *off* the edge of the bank into certain peril.

It is these times that I wonder what in the world I will do, when God calls her home.

Dr. Susan Bailey

Mother Rowland, I know I have not known you as long as some but longer than others. It is a pleasure to know you. I pray that your years and wisdom continue to be a blessing to me and others. You are a blessing. May God bless you with many years to come.

Gwendolyn Walker
Seasoned Saints

HAPPY 99th BIRTHDAY Rev. Rowland!

As you celebrate your 99th Birthday, I pray that you will have a blessed and enjoyable day. Thanks for being a great teacher and inspiration in my life. You are never too busy to listen, encourage, and pray for others no matter what time you are called.

You have truly made a difference in the world and especially in the lives of those around you and your Word of Faith family. May the love and kindness you have sown to others be returned to you tenfold.

I pray that you continue to be reminded of Psalms 19:16:

> *"With long life will I satisfy him and show Him my salvation."*

HAPPY 99th BIRTHDAY!

Your Sister in Christ Jesus,
Mattie Copeland

Thank God for Mother Rowland

One of her favorite sayings is "Thank God for Jesus!" And I would like to begin my tribute with Thank God for Mother Rowland!

I have been a member of Word of Faith for four years and always use to rush home after first service. Then one day my friend, Sylvia Chambless, invited me to come to Sunday School – The Women of Acts class. When I sat there listening to this seasoned, wise, godly, humble woman teach us the word of God and loving every minute of it and making sure we understood what she was teaching, I was hooked and instantly fell in love with Mother Rowland's teaching and eagerness to share the word of God!

I love Mother Rowland personally and as she always says, she will not die, she will live Eternally!

Happy Birthday Mother and may God Bless you with many more to come.

Love,
Stephanie Williams
A member of the Women of Acts Sunday School class

She loves Jesus! She loves people!

If I were asked for a description of Reverend Mother Emma Rowland, my response would be as follows:

She is a woman of character, diminutive in physical stature yet colossal in spiritual stature, whose faithful leadership always begins and ends with prayer.

We met at Word of Faith Family Worship Center East Point, GA in 1995 in Sunday School. Mother Rowland was the Sunday School Teacher. What an anointed Bible Teacher! It was easy to discern that she loved God's Word and that she loved teaching it. Our class flourished in biblical knowledge. She faithfully continues to teach the 'Women of Acts' class today.

Additionally, Mother Rowland volunteered as Leader of the Church's 'Clean-up Ministry'. Every Saturday, for many years, she guided her small crew of volunteers in cleaning up the church. (I even assisted a few times.) What humility and joy can be achieved from doing what is considered lowly tasks.

Last, but not least, Reverend Mother Rowland has been the leader of the Tuesday night 'Women's Daily Walk Ministry'. This Ministry is an indepth biblical study for women to learn God's Word in order that they may apply it successfully to the everyday experiences of life and thereby mature victoriously.

This Woman of God, at the age of ninety-eight is enjoying numerous latter-day blessings. Several years ago, the Holy Spirit led me and others to approach Mother (individually) about picking her up for Church, Doctor's appointments, etc. At the time, she was driving her Cadillac everywhere she wanted to go. But, after going to the Lord in prayer, she agreed. I know it wasn't easy for her to relinquish driving because she is a very strong independent woman of God who still lives alone in her own home. God blessed her to be able to sell her Cadillac immediately!

For the past several years, she has enjoyed traveling to Chicago, Colorado, and New York; places she has confessed to me that she had always desired to go and never thought she would. All of these trips were gifts. Praise God through whom all Blessings flow!!!

What a Blessing the life of this woman displays to all! She loves Jesus!!! She loves people!!! Her quiet demeanor is an example for us all (both male and female; old and young). Reverend Mother Emma Rowland is truly a doer of the Word and not a hearer only! Her wisdom always leads you to

God's Word. She is full of wisdom from the Word, yet is still meek and teachable with a witty sense of humor.

At 98 years old, there are only eyeglasses and a walking cane ... Praise God!

How Blessed I am to be able to call Reverend Mother Emma Rowland, Teacher and Friend!

Nedra Holman

Tribute to Mother (Reverend) Emma Rowland

I'm honored to have this opportunity to share what Mother Rowland means to me. She has set an example for me to follow and continues to inspire me in my leadership position as Coordinator and Advisor of the Seasoned Saints Ministry. She is also a member of the Seasoned Saints Ministry and served for two years as Coordinator and Advisor in 2000-2001.

She is a blessing to the ministry and brings a sense of calmness just by her presence. We continue to call upon her as speaker, teacher, counselor, and advisor. Mother Rowland has been our keynote speaker for many occasions. She gives joy, hope and compassion.

Mother Rowland possesses all the qualities of a Godly woman. She preaches and teaches the gospel of Christ Jesus and lives a submitted life. She's a prayer warrior and worship is a way of life for her. At 99 years of age, her mind is still strong and she is content as she continues her journey for the Lord.

Let me say, in closing, in a world that is sometimes dark and ungodly, Mother Rowland shines bright as Matthew 5:16 instructs,

> *"Let your light shine before men in such a way that they may see your good works, and glorify your Father who is in heaven".*

May God bless you and keep you in his loving care.
Love,
Florence Jackson, *Coordinator, Seasoned Saints Ministry*

Her Supportive Spirit is Legendary

Some tasks are difficult and daunting and others like this one are pleasant and joyful.

To be able to make comments about someone that you love is one of the best feelings that my wife and I have had the pleasure of doing.

Let me start by saying that we are all on an incredible journey through this wonder-filled life. On the journey you will meet some people that are to be remembered and some that you may hope to forget. Well it seems that Mother Rowland is in the former category.

She will never be forgotten.

My wife and I agree that Mother is *W*ISDOM

                *O*UTSPOKEN

                *M*ENTOR *(WOMAN)*

                *A*NGEL

                *N*EGOTIATOR

All rolled up into a small and, might I add, very neat and well-dressed package of LOVE.

My wife says that Mother is that ever present angel that you want to be on your shoulder at all times to keep your spirit encouraged.

There are always kind words and never that feeling of what just happened when you leave her. She will make her thoughts and plans clear so that if you misunderstood what she said, that was your misfortune.

Mother's supportive spirit is legendary.

My wife recalls the death of her mother as one of those times when she really didn't expect to see Mother.

The Church, where the funeral service was held, had some challenges with stairs and or boundaries that we would not have expected Mother to handle, but who did we see smiling and full of love for the family but Mother Rowland.

It's those things that you remember and never forget about her.

We call her the grandmother that always shows that she cares. When you love the Lord as much as she does you can't help but love others.

Mother and I had a conversation the other day and I had to stop and look at her real good to be sure that she wasn't having an out of body experience. She knew in detail all of what I was talking about before I could finish my introduction.

I felt that I had talked with my Mother, my Wife, my Mentor, my best friend, my spiritual advisor, and my Guardian Angel all in the same person. WOW.

We love you Mother
Deacon Johnnie & Beverly Simmons

Happy Birthday to the best mother we know. We hope God keeps giving you Love, Life and blessings. We want to be like you when we grow up. We love your teaching and it has changed our lives more than you will ever know.

Love you
Gloria & Elizabeth

Phenomenal: Highly Extraordinary or Exceptional.

That's Mother Rowland. Our meeting at Daily Walk for Women in 1994 at Word of Faith Family Worship Center was meant to be.

You are everything good, honest, and kind.

May the peace of God be with you always.

I thank God every day for you.

He knows whose best for me and that is YOU.

I love you,
Velma E. Watkins

She is Amazing!

There is a Power of the Spirit that so richly resides in this Wonderful Woman of God. Almost 20 years ago the Lord availed my heart to this anointed vessel.

Every opportunity to be taught by her took me to a new level of faith on the journey. Every hug reassured me – even seated with her in the Presbytery, brings me joy.

No one can say, "Hi Beautiful" like Reverend Mother Emma Rowland. It energizes me with unexplainable blessings, because the "beauty" that she speaks of is not on the outside. She is prophesying with salutations; reminding us of the Beauty for Ashes that only God Himself gives freely.

I truly love and respect our Reverend Mother Rowland.

She is amazing!
Dr. Jane Render
Pastor Of Membership Development
Word of Faith Family Worship Cathedral

She is a Gentle Soul

I am writing to give testimony of how Mom Rowland and I came to be mother and daughter. In 2005, I was at church service at Word of Faith. The announcements flashed across the screen and it listed the sick and shut in members. Mom Rowland's name came across the screen and immediately the Holy Spirit instructed me to go pray with her. I went to inquire about where she was and immediately after service I went to the hospital where she was. When I walked in her room and introduced myself, immediately it was love at first sight. I anointed her room and prayed with her and she told me that I was an angel sent to her by God. From that day forward Mom Rowland and I became one. My mother died when I was 17, and though no one could ever replace her, Mom Rowland filled a void that I had been missing for a long time. She is gentle, easy to talk to and most importantly, she never judges! Mom and I would go visit other churches together and one service holds so clear in my mind still today. We went to this service on a Friday night and when we got there we were ushered to the first row. During the service, the minister called Mom Rowland out and began to prophesy to her. The minister told mother that God said that she can come home when she is ready to come home. He said that you have been faithful to me for so long and that you can come home when you are ready. Every year that goes by and mom has another birthday, I praise God and I say to myself, she is not ready yet. She is a mother to many and has a humility in her heart that is so refreshing. Mom is a gentle soul who has unconditional love towards

God's people. She is a true example of what a "Christian" should look like. My life has truly been enriched and blessed with the person of Mother Emma J. Rowland who is a true inspiration and mentor in my life! I will love you always Mom Rowland.

Vivian Toney

A Collide with Royalty

By Cynthia Harper

Though it appeared to be a typical Sunday, it was anything but. I was oblivious to the fact that on that day, my destiny would collide with royalty and my life would be forever changed. It was the day I connected to Mother Emma Rowland through a ministry called PUSH, Pray Until Something Happens. The question posed was, "Would you like to participate in the 24x7 prayer team, where we partner you with someone to pray the vision of the Pastor?" My response, "Sure I love to pray, intercession is my calling." I now know, linking together with you, a giant, genuine, gentle spirit was sent to guide and walk with me during some difficult seasons. Prayer went forth and I learned to listen for the voice of God through your intercession.

During our many breakfasts, dinners and countless engagements, often times you say, "Cynthia, trust God, He already knows the answer." Recounting the days of laughter yet remembering the days of tears, you allowed me to be free to share my truths without judgements regardless of the topic. I love the fact that I could totally be vulnerable in your presence, yet inspired afterwards. You have no desire to hurt, but to correct in love. Your ability to always look for God and to pray before you offered up any opinion has taught me not to speak too quickly. You are amazing, Mother Rowland; there is never a civil, social nor political issue of which you are not aware. Your intelligence is equally matched in world views as it is with biblical truths.

Sitting at your feet has always brought calm to my soul; sitting at your table, drinking coffee and enjoying a southern breakfast feeds my body and your wise answers to the myriad of questions I often call you, with put my mind at rest. I love so many things about you, but the one thing I love the most is you are confidential. You are the epitome of truth and a woman who truly seeks after God's heart. There is a biblical text which reads, "before honour is humility". That is who you are! Your knowledge has not given you a false sense of pride, it has humbled you, therefore many get to see your exaltation. You have been bestowed great honor from people and organizations because your walk is your talk. Speaking of walking, that steep hill leading up and down at your home, is more than a notion.

"Congratulations for climbing it successfully". I am certain, it is God, who graces you to do it.

I think about when you were in the hospital and I tried relentlessly to find your room. Leaving without seeing you was out of the question. I have to admit, I was scared of what I would find. However I walked into a brave, strong and content environment, where you had set an atmosphere of praise. You greeted with, "Come on over here and give me a kiss a girl." Whatever tried to attack your health had to flee because you knew your God as a healer. Shortly there afterwards, you were released and in God's perfect timing, you were healed eager to teach the women whom God has assigned to you. I have garnered so much wisdom from you, I could create a set of encyclopedias, compartmentalized by alpha-numeric sequence. I promise I could start with A and end with Z, scribing a plethora of things others and I have learned.

Mother Rowland you are known for your knowledge and how to rightfully divide the word of God, but I would be remiss not to speak of your green thumb. Your plants and lawn are beautiful. Their fullness, color and longevity prove that you spend quality time on them. As they cascade your porch, they add life to your home. Just as you have pruned me in areas, you keep your plants in shape. I have not mastered my plants yet, but it's on my bucket list. (smile)

I am always inspired by your travels and how you continue to educate and expose yourself to some of the world's greatest teachings and institutions. You have been an exemplary leader and age has not defied you, but has given you an even greater courage. It was in your nineties when you started to use the computer. What an accomplishment! While I know you loved your grandmother who taught you so much during childhood, it's obvious your latter is greater than your former. What an awesome life you have. Your tenacious spirit is infectious and God can count on you to faithfully carry out His will.

Without a shadow of a doubt, the world is a better place because you are in it. You add value to people, conversations, community, etc. Your character is unmatched and you have a sense of humor. When you find something funny, it's cute how you place your hand over your mouth and drop your head. You are in touch with your human side but you always remain holy. When you decided to follow Jesus, you did and in my presence, you have never wavered. You are a trailblazer who has set a high-standard. When they told you "NO" you could not preach the gospel, you told God YES, and you have continued throughout the decades. I can't thank you enough for helping me with all the lessons for my youth group along with food and snacks for the children, Sunday school lessons, speeches, etc. You never ceased to care for those around you because you are a builder of people.

My adoration for you runs deep because we share multiple similarities which jointly fit us together. Things like singing the old hundred songs my grandmother loved so much, you and my mother share the same birthdate, and ultimately your heart to serve God and people. Those are just a few of the experiences which drew me closer to you, leaving me with unspeakable joy. Mother Rowland, so many people love you and I admire your family for sharing you, with us. I realize their openness to share you is due in part to the way you reared them. You make room for all of us but never compromise them. You are rich and have so much to give. Though you are petite in statute your heart is really BIG. I thank God for allowing our paths to cross; to know I have the pleasure of being in your presence is amazing. You are a tremendous blessing to the body of Christ.

Writing about our relationship is easy, because it's true, preordained, and it had to happen for prophecy to be fulfilled. You are doing as the Lord has commanded, showing unconditional love, steering me to a place of greatness; teaching me things to come and sharing your mantle of holiness. Though I don't proclaim to be completely there, my journey will be much easier for knowing you. Rest assured, I have confidence to climb my mountain and will remain steadfast, immovable and always abounding. You bring out the best in me and I proudly sit at your feet, though I don't measure up.

You are approaching the beautiful age of ninety-nine. Biblically, the number nine symbolizes fruit of the spirit; divine completeness from the Father, as well as the hour of prayer. When I look at the latter, I am reminded that this is how we came to know each other, through PRAYER.

Mother Rowland, this is not flattery, but a privilege to honor you. With all sincerity, I view you as royalty.

Cynthia Harper

A Woman who Serves (Period)

To My Inspiration, Mother Emma Rowland,

I am pleased to be a part of such an awesome memoir. In the years that I have known you, I have come to the conclusion that you are a "woman who serves" (period).

I thoroughly enjoy your dynamic conversations, encouragement, wisdom and knowledge. It is an honor and privilege to serve with you in the Seasoned Saints Ministry (and I've often attended your Sunday school class). Since serving with you, I have developed a deeper understanding of true love and worship. As someone who has been committed to God as long as you have, I feel like a superstar being in your presence and learning from you all these years – even when you didn't realize I was watching and listening. You continually teach us Kingdom principles by the way you live your life, and you have a unique way about you that compels people to want to live a Godly life.

I admire your leadership, your guidance, your tenacity, your faith and the many other qualities that I've experienced by hanging around you. I have never met such a woman!

Much love and admiration,
Naomi Williams

She Wears a Crown of Glory

The hoary head is a crown of glory, if it be found in the way of righteousness.
Proverbs 16:31

In the truest sense – treowe: real not counterfeit, genuine is the proverb – the hoary head is a crown of glory if it be found in the way of righteousness.

It is Sunday morning and there I see a four foot two inch woman walking to the middle of the pulpit, during our devotional service, and I smile. I have an innate honor for those who have travelled this life before me. That is to say those yet living and breathing, and with greyish hair. You know, those individuals who are not too many years shy of a century. There she was, walking gracefully and praying fervently with certainty, soundness, and love. Again, I smiled. I would see her in this capacity from time to time.

One day I decided to attend a Sunday school class and, to my surprise, she was teaching on that Sunday. During the class I went from listening, to *eagerly* listening. My heart began to yearn for more of what I was hearing. I was so grateful, full of joy, and divinely thankful.

When the Word of God is taught by someone who is full of the Holy Ghost, it leaves a divine impact on the hearer. To see her fervency about The Lord, in her age group, reminded me of my grandmother and I was literally blessed just by being in her presence. To God be all of the glory. Whenever she opened her mouth and taught the class I was so blessed, time after time. This went on occasionally for about three years.

One day we were chatting and again, I felt so blessed that I asked her if I could come to visit her and she gracefully accepted my request. The day finally came for me to go visit and we sat and talked. It was the type of conversing that blesses your soul. Anyhow, I had to go to the ladies room and I am the type of person that pays attention to details and appreciates cleanliness. As I am about to wash my hands I could see the rust on the toilet and sink from years of use; but it was clean! As we chatted, she told me she had been living in that house for over fifty years. Her house was clean. To be in her 90's and still clean and cleaning — that is my caliber of woman. Our visit was such a sweet fellowship of communion by The Spirit. As I was about to leave, I asked her if we could pray and she responded "How can we not pray?" I was moved with passion and admiration because she was speaking my language. It was at that moment that I realized that she loves Jesus just as much as I do.

Here and there I would call to say hello, to chat, or to see if she needed anything. For the few times she said yes, it was truly an honor to assist her. I felt privileged.

Her presence was such a blessing that I wanted my extended family, that lives in another state, to experience her and her, in turn, to experience them. If I introduce people that I know to each other, I like for both individuals and/or parties to experience the "best" of what I know about each person and I had the desire for that to happen. I acknowledged The Lord in my desire and in His own time and season He made it happen. My desire was fulfilled. She experienced my family at their best and they in turn experienced the essence of who she is. It was a blessed communion.

When she speaks about The Lord I can see His strength rise up in her. I'm in my 30s and she is in her 90s and He has captured both of our hearts. The passion I have in my 30s, she has in her 90s and I love it because she is still following Jesus Christ. Amen! There is a "look" that comes with living righteously; I call it a "Holy Glow". It is that Holy light, as a result of Holy living, that shines so brightly through her.

To also see how The Lord takes care of her is yet astonishing. The fact that she does not drive anymore, yet, when she has a desire to go somewhere or do something, The Lord sends someone to answer her desire every time is totally amazing. She really reminds me of my dear, dear mother because The Lord takes care of her in like manner. Her cleanliness reminds me of my mother, as does her soundness of mind and unwavering faith in God.

Jesus Christ is what is common amongst us and for me to witness that same peace, passion, and love in a person during the latter years of their life is the very essence of The Word of God and my experience in it. *Blessed is the hoary head, if it be found in the way of righteousness* ... Amen, Amen, Amen.

To God be all the glory.

This is she, Mother Emma Rowland – it is The Lord's doing and it is marvelous in our eyes.

Tondalaya Woods

She Loves the Lord

I met Mother Rowland while attending a WOF picnic at Welcome All Park. She reminded me of my grandmother. The next time I saw her was in a Sunday school class. Then we met again at Daily Walk while still at the East Point location.

I remember sitting outside one Tuesday (in the summer time) having our Daily Walk class, because the church was closed. I knew then how much she loved the Word.

How I came into being Mother Rowland's Armor Barrier at the church's new location was this. I used to work in the kitchen ministry with Melody who was the head of the Hospitality Ministry. She asked since Julia was going back to school and wouldn't be able to escort Mother on Thursday's, she asked me if I would and you know the rest.

Going over to Mother Rowland's house studying the Word and praying and listening to some of things that has happened in her past, has encouraged me not to give up. Not only me, but others as well.

I heard her say, "What does the word say?" when someone is talking to her about their life challenges.

One Tuesday evening while escorting her to the car and we got outside and there was Deacon Getter, she took his arm and said to me, "Sorry, when a man offers to escort you, you gotta take it." LOL

When walking her to someone else's car and she gets in, I say Bible(check)pocketbook(check). She said, "I wouldn't want you to have to come back out tonight and bring me my Bible." LOL

Another thing is, she loves to go. One Saturday I was out and about and I thought about the church was having the annual picnic the same day. I called Mother, asked her if she wanted to go and I pick her up in about 30 minutes. When I walked in the house, I saw the vaccum cleaner in the middle of the floor. "Do you want me to put it up?" She said, "When you called and said go," I left it there and got dressed," LOL.

Mother Rowland has made me see that I'm not living for just me, myself and my family but for what God would have me to do for others.

My faith has increased since being around her. We need to be steadfast in our faith and to know God is sovereign. She told me one day when I was trying to get her to change a sweater out (which I thought didn't look good), she said she was trying to make sure her soul was right with God.

When she is in pain, she doesn't complain about it. She says go while you can, just keep moving.

I've learned from Mother that some things don't need to be talked about, but prayed about.

It's so much a pleasure to be a part of her family. Thanks family for letting me be a part of you.

Love you,
Leola 'Le' Butler
Armor Bearer

A Mighty Woman of God

Reverend Rowland is a true follower of our Lord and Savior Jesus Christ. God continues to use her to draw many to Him. At age 99, she continues her legacy of *love, commitment, dedication and perseverance*. Why do I say that's part of her legacy? It's because of the following:

Love: *1 Corinthians 13:4: Love is patient, love is kind. It does not envy, it does not boast, it is not proud.* Reverend Rowland displays these Godly qualities as our Sunday School teacher in Women of Acts Class.

Commitment: *Proverbs 16:3: Commit your work to the Lord, and your plans will be established.* Reverend Rowland has preached the good news for decades and has impacted many.

Dedication: *1 Peter 1:13: Wherefore gird up the loins of your mind, be sober, and hope to the end for the grace that is to be brought unto you at the revelation of Jesus Christ.* Reverend Rowland is leaving large footprints for us to follow and has dedicated her life to the work of building the Kingdom of God.

Perseverance: *James 1:12: Blessed is the man who remains steadfast under trial, for when he has stood the test he will receive the crown of life, which God has promised to those who love him.* HER CROWN AWAITS HER. I remember so many times when Reverend Rowland would say to us "I just love Jesus". She is both ordinary and extraordinary… a gentle giant.

I'm deeply honored to be one of many to share her impact on my life and to express what a blessing she has been to me. I have verbally told her how much I'm blessed when speaking with her and just learning from her over the years, and my feelings only continue to grow in admiration for her. She has inspired me to live a surrendered life and to allow the Holy Spirit to lead me.

My prayer is that God will continue to bless this awesome woman of God as she continues her service to Him.

Love and blessings,
Mae H. Battle

"Blessed are the Righteous that put their trust in God."

The Glory of God surrounds our dear Sister, Mother, Minister, Teacher and more.

I have always admired Mother Rowland since meeting her in 2003. When I began visiting "Word of Faith", I attended her Sunday school class at the Sam's Building, which is now the Epi-Center. After joining "Word of Faith" Church in September 2003 and taking the required classes for membership, I became involved with other ministries and never returned to Minister Rowland's class. I have always enjoyed Sunday school, but I became part of a ministry that I had never served on before that required more classes and we met at the same class time as Sunday school. I do get to see Minister Rowland in our "Seasoned Saints" meetings where she is a devotional leader. She always brings forth very inspiring words. The same is true when she prays at Worship service on Sunday mornings. She speaks truth and is a blessing to all that know her.

> *I pray her 99th birthday will be her best ever and that the "joy of the Lord" be her strength. May the joy of the Lord enfold her, keeping her safe and in good health.*

Happy 99th Birthday Reverend Mother Rowland.

Sister Alice Robinson Evans
Word of Faith, Sister In Christ
Seasoned Saint, Intercessor

I have always loved Mother Rowland ever since I met her and since I became a member of the Seasoned Saints she has been a person that I look up to and is someone that I admire and love. She is a wonderful person.

All my love,
Lena Barnes

Reverend Emma Rowland,

I greatly appreciate the Godly example you represent in Word of Faith Family Worship Cathedral. I celebrate you along with many others whose lives have been touched by your love, joy and compassion. Just knowing you has enriched my life and I thank God for your powerful Godly influence over many years.

May God continue to bless you as much as you bless others.

Love,
Bettye Hunter

My Dear Mother Rowland,

It is a joy and a delight to know such a Godly woman. I cannot find the perfect words to thank you for being such a thoughtful and caring person. Every time I have talked with you, you always seem to know just what to say to meet my needs (not only me, but many others). Your kindness, wisdom and love for people is such a part of your nature, and the positive impact that you have on others will be the legacy that you'll leave.

Mother Rowland, I want you to know that your generous, loving and Godly spirit has touched my life more than once; and although "thank you" is a phrase you hear very often, I want to say it again. I also want you to know that I love and appreciate you very much.

My prayer is that God will continue to bless you and keep you in His care.

Your sister in Christ,
Sis. Blanche Mills

Time with Mother Rowland

I have been a member of Word of Faith since 1997 and Mother Emma Rowland has always been an encouraging source of wisdom to anyone that would listen.

In November of 2012, the Lord put it on my heart to set up a meeting with Mother Rowland. The purpose of the meeting was just to sit with her and to record some of the wisdom that she has to offer concerning life, ministry, and family. I initially met with her alone and was tremendously blessed by our time together. Then, once I mentioned it to Pastor (Christopher) Boyd, he asked me if I recorded it ... ☺. Since I did not, I suggested meeting with Mother Rowland once again and invited both Pastor Jose (Adames) and Brother Paul (Patrick) to sit in. The second time, (about 2 weeks later), was just as much of a blessing as the first.

Mother Rowland talked about her childhood, being the 7th of 9 children and how her grandmother wound up raising her. One of the greatest things that Mother Rowland's grandmother did for her was to teach her the word of God and ignite a hunger for the Bible. Some of the strongest messages that I received from our time together was that the Lord gave Mother Rowland a dream when she was young and in that dream God told her the world was her pulpit. She was to read and study the Word to show herself approved unto God .... (2 Timothy 2:15a). She said that the Lord has helped her not to be lonely because He (God) has been a Mother and Father to her. She said that the scripture that God focused her on when she was converted many years ago came from John 6:36-44. Mother Rowland mentioned to us that her favorite 2 songs are "Amazing Grace" and "Blessed Assurance". We actually took a praise break and sang some of Blessed Assurance. It was a fantastic time of fellowship.

Mother Rowland spoke specifically and said to us to go and teach the gospel. She admonished us to remember our Call and preach and teach the Gospel in season and out. It felt like a commissioning of a wise elder (a female Paul) to two spiritual mentees (Pastor Jose and I as "Timothys").

Apart from this personal time of counsel and teaching, I am very thankful every time that I moderate our Sunday services and Mother Rowland is the designated prayer for that day. In addition to hearing her come humbly before the Throne of Grace, I am always honored to walk her to the front of the pulpit. I count it a privilege and joy to listen to the prayers of a Seasoned Woman of God who is running her race with God in humility, with Grace and the Favor of God obviously on her side.

I love and am thankful for Rev. Emma Rowland.

Rev. Charles Houston
Associate Pastor of Counseling
Word of Faith Family Worship Cathedral

A Woman of Royalty

Mother Rowland sat down and gave me the privilege to share my gift P.I.N. Power-In-Names with her one Sunday. Through the Holy Spirit, we have the ability to enrich peoples lives by revealing the power in and giving them awareness of their God given name. Every person needs to know their purpose and identity in the Body of Christ. Your name is a powerful tool as you develop and grow in Christ. The two major gifts you will experience after we speak over your name are prophecy and word of knowledge. You will have a better understanding with confirmation toward your destiny in life.

I shared with Mother Rowland a prophecy of how she came over many mountains. It was a rough childhood growing up. A lot of people really do not know her story. She has a mothering, nurturing nature always caring for others. She has always been a fighter for righteousness. Intercessor, a praying woman filled with wisdom because of her faithfulness. Her life and legacy will touch seven generations without a doubt. Her dreams have placed a mantle of grace with a double anointing for healing. She has been gifted to touch generations as she is a woman of royalty.

That is what I saw in her name. We need millions more just like her.

Evangelist Dr. Curtis Minter
www.power-in-names.com

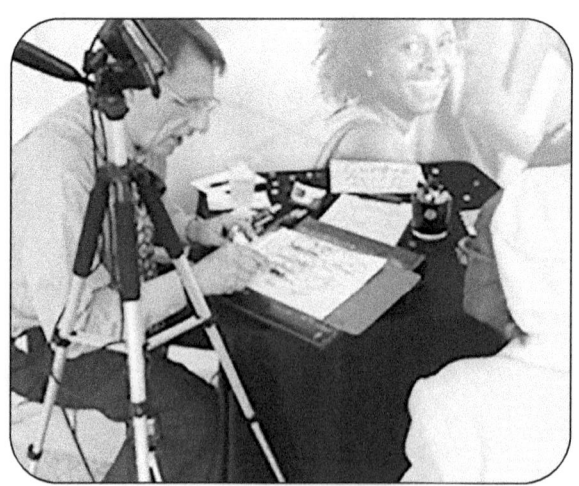

The Rowland Report
By Brother Paul Patrick, III
WOF Sunday School Ministry Leader

Reverend Emma Jane Rowland, who we affectionately refer to as Mother Rowland, has inspired so many individuals in the Sunday School Ministry at Word of Faith Family Worship Cathedral; it is somewhat difficult to even associate a number to the lives she has touched over the years. Mother Rowland responded to the call to serve as a Sunday School teacher when the church first started. In 1992, Bishop Dale C. Bronner organized the Sunday School department. Several classes were established. The Adult Women's class was one of those classes and Mother Emma Rowland was identified as one of the teachers. The teachers were asked to select names for the classes. After prayer, the Lord placed it on Mother's Rowland's heart that the ladies in the class were to be active in service for The Lord or Women of Action and as a result, the name of the class became "Women of Acts".

In 2015, at the young age of 98, Mother Rowland is still serving in this capacity. Mother Rowland recognized and accepted the fact that God does not speak about retirement in the Bible. If He has called you to teach, you should continue to teach until He calls you to do something else. Well, Mother Rowland is still teaching and still inspiring brothers and sisters to get connected and stay connected to Christ. Since Mother Rowland is such a powerful teacher, men who join the Sunday School Ministry are strongly encouraged to sit in on Women of Acts class in order to hear words of wisdom and to witness her style of teaching. There are not too many classes designed for women that men would gladly attend!!! With Mother Rowland leading such a class, men are happy to join the class and participate periodically.

Mother Rowland would probably not consider herself as a Master Teacher but to the Sunday School Ministry, she is definitely a Master Teacher. A great teacher accepts the fact that they are always a "student". Of all the teachers that have been trained at WOF, there is one person that continues to go thru all the training getting refreshed each and every time. If Mother Rowland is aware of a training session, she will be present and accounted for in the class. Mother Rowland continues to take the position that she does not know everything and is willing to learn and grow. What an Awesome Example!!!!

In 2009, Mother Rowland's words of wisdom sparked a change in the Sunday School Ministry when she coined the phrase "Sunday School is all about Learning a Lesson". A simple yet powerful description of Sunday School stated by Mother Rowland reminds each of us of the purpose and objective of Sunday School. Mother Rowland would often say "…it does not take a long time to teach a lesson. All you need is 30 minutes. It does not take all day. "

Mother Rowland's words of wisdom also inspired the WOF Sunday School Ministry to unveil a 5 week study called the Rowland Report - "Simple Lessons About God" that will help students to fully understand the 5W's of God: 1) Who Is God? 2) What are the different names of God? 3) When should I start my walk with God? 4) Where you will see God Move? and 5) Why should we join God's Team? Each lesson within this curriculum is intentionally designed to be taught within a 30-45 minute time frame. This 5 week study will be offered at least twice a year. During the development of this curriculum, we asked Mother Rowland to create the 1st lesson. At the time, Mother Rowland did not realize the lesson she crafted would be documented and placed in such a curriculum. Capturing Mother Rowland's words of wisdom and passion

for the Lord will truly touch the hearts of so many brothers and sisters who desire to learn more about God. The WOF Sunday School Ministry prays that each person that participates in this class will be led into a stronger relationship with Christ with hopes that they will receive a revelation of God's direction and purpose for their life.

I personally had the honor and privilege of hearing Mother Rowland share aspects of a dream and how she was led to Word of Faith. God gave her a dream about being in a wonderful and beautiful garden. She was led not to the front of the garden where many of the large flowers were blooming, but to the back of the garden. Being in the front of the garden noted being in a large church while being in the back indicated plans to be in a smaller church. Mother Rowland was being led to a place she would serve behind the scenes. This was during the time God led Bishop Bronner to start Word of Faith Family Worship Cathedral and formulate a Sunday School Ministry. Since this time, WOF has grown to over 20,000 members. The Word teaches us to "despise not small beginnings". God used Mother Rowland in more ways than we realize here at WOF. God planted Mother Rowland in the Sunday School Ministry to blossom and it has been a true blessing.

God has blessed me to have a number of dreams that involved Mother Rowland. One in particular pertained to a period where Mother Rowland and I were at a party in a large facility. Mother Rowland appeared to be in her early to mid 30's, beautiful and with a gorgeous dress. We sat and danced and had a great time together. The following Sunday, I shared this dream with Mother Rowland. She had on the same color dress and looked much younger on this particular day just as in my dream. I'm so grateful to have the opportunity to serve (i.e. to dance) with Mother Rowland during my time in the Sunday School Ministry. She has shared words of wisdom, provided direction, and encouraged not just myself and my family, but the entire Sunday School family. Words cannot express the joy she has brought to brothers and sisters that walk through the halls of Sunday School.

During a recent poll, Sunday School servants were asked to provide one word that describes Mother Rowland. A flood of responses were received and here a few examples to share:

- Faithful
- Incredible
- Angel
- Holy
- Godly
- Passionate
- Sage
- Matriarch
- Wise
- Experienced
- Strong
- Steadfast
- Prophet

God has planted each of us in a garden just as Mother Rowland. For the past few years, we have shared that this is the season to capture words of wisdom, experiences, and all the lessons from someone like Mother Rowland. We are grateful in the Sunday School Ministry to have the honor and privilege to serve alongside an awesome Woman of God who has such passion for the word of God and love for Jesus Christ.

Emma Jane Rowland

Emma Jane Rowland

www.ingramcontent.com/pod-product-compliance
Lightning Source LLC
Chambersburg PA
CBHW062218080426
42734CB00010B/1942